THE ENERGY

of

MONEY

How to Understand and Quantum Leap Your Relationship with Money Using Metaphysical Insights

Lynn M. Scheurell

MIZRAHI PRESS

The Energy of Money:
How to Understand and Quantum Leap Your
Relationship with Money Using Metaphysical Insights

ISBN-13: 978-0-9801550-4-4 (paperback)

Limit of Liability/Disclaimer of Warranty
While the author has used their best efforts in preparing this report, they make no representation or warranties with respect to the accuracy or completeness of the contents and specifically disclaim any implied warranties. The advice and strategies contained herein may not be suitable for your situation. You should consult with a professional where appropriate. The author shall not be liable for any loss of profit or any other commercial damages, including but not limited to special, incidental, consequential or other damages.

Published by Mizrahi Press
A Division of Creative Catalyst LLC
MyCreativeCatalyst.com

*With gratitude for a lifetime of teachings
around money, abundance and prosperity,
and for my clients who shared their experiences
with me through our work together.*

Contents

How To Make Friends With Your Money As an Entrepreneur   193

Author's Note

One of the reasons this book is so important is because self-help techniques don't always help and, in fact, are useless if they are painful to apply. For example, think about the last time you sat down to write out your budget, document your expenses or write down where the time in your day went… these are all common, valuable ways to understand yourself better. However, they are challenging to implement when you have blocks to them (and if you are not doing these kinds of activities, you probably have subconscious blocks in the way). There is a disincentive to follow conventional wisdom because there is not enough immediate pay off for investing time in it. Additionally, that kind of education may never pay off, because the block (when not addressed) will prevent you from upgrading your relationship with money anyway.

So now you have the pain of your challenge, compounded with the pain of the so-called solution(s)… which means there is a lot of pain energy now present in your conscious awareness (not to mention all that is hiding unconsciously), and no real tools to clear it. Often the lack of clarity in understanding your relationship with money comes from places within you that need healing. And, because this book 'spoke' to you, you may not even know what that even means but you DO know things can be different with you and money.

If there is a resistance to change AND there is an attachment to what is familiar (whether or not it is dysfunctional and not working), there is something that is inviting a healing (which is asking for change). Accordingly, there might be an inherent resistance to anything external directing you to change, which can include your own messages if perceived as an outside source trying to change you in ways you do not want.

Remember, there is no outside source creating change—instead, you call in situations that prompt contrast between what you want and what you currently have to get your attention so you can create change.

Another less direct form of resistance is when you believe you already know something, you won't question what you know AND you won't likely be able to see what is new or unfamiliar that is outside what you already know. So what was once a boundary you saw as serving you in a positive way becomes a limitation that constricts your perceptions about money.

This book is intended to be a resource to help you explore your relationship with money so you can consciously upgrade it, which will give you new freedom (and likely attract, earn, generate and keep more money).

Quick caveat: does reading this book mean you will get rich quick or have more money? I don't know and cannot promise that outcome for you. What I can promise is you will have new tools and resources to understand yourself better in your relationship to and with money. This is one aspect of self-mastery, which is an ever-evolving pursuit.

With the understanding that this is about your self-discovery, let's begin.

How to Get the Most from This Book

This book is a compilation of several works that I had written over many years as I discovered tools to ever-deepen clarity around money. You should know I'm not an economist or financial advisor or have a financial background. What I do offer you is a way to approach self-mastery through gaining compelling clarity.

My prime directive since the age of 17 is to activate potential. The name of my business likely says it best—I am a Creative Catalyst. I invite and incite transformation through self-discovery. Since 1998, that's been my business. I've worked with thousands of people at this point, often by helping my wonderful and amazing clients see their own value. It's my honor and privilege to share forward what I've learned as a result. At heart, I am a teacher.

My intention in writing this book is to give you new ways to explore your relationship with money, beginning with what money actually means… because when something is about the money, it's never about the money. And yet, money is the result, the symptom and the means of one's understanding made material.

One of the most interesting things about money is that it isn't *just* money—it's survival in today's world. You experience the world is differently based on whether you have money or not. When you do not have enough money, it triggers core survival thinking and behavior. As Maslow said in his Hierarchy of Needs, you must address your needs in order of priority to experience higher needs. This means when you don't have enough money, you (typically) cannot think about creating art, helping someone else in your community or pursuing your self-actualization goals. Money enables you to experience a richer life on more than the material level.

This book is structured in sections of content. You don't need to read it in order—you can choose what section appeals most to you and start there. In many sections, there are exercises designed to help you gain personal insight. In doing those, remember there is no right or wrong; instead, this is simply about surfacing clarity.

Once you have clarity, you have choice. When you exercise choice, you change your experience.

Money Paradigms and Neutralizing Saboteurs

Money Measures Exchange

Money is a symbolic measure and system that measures the exchange of energy between people. Money is very literal—it does not judge where it should go and who should have it. Your money paradigms are systems of beliefs you developed over time about how you predictably understand and relate with money, including your expectations, habits, and behaviors.

In general, the money exchange system as we know it is about paying for services provided (not even for services delivered). For example, we pay doctors for cures from illness vs. prevention and maintenance of wellness, which is the real desired outcome of healthcare.

People create opportunities by packaging their assets and resources into solutions and providing services other people want, need and are willing to pay money for to solve a problem or meet a need. To have the money to pay for those solutions, customers had to understand their own energetic access points to attracting, creating, and having money.

And therein lies the source of most dysfunctional money belief systems… it is in the money exchange cycle. People ascribe their particular expectations, emotional needs or projections about their thoughts, needs and wants into the money exchange and, when those do not occur as expected, the cycle of exchange becomes laden with unfulfilled expectation, negative emotional need or other energetic parasites that don't belong in the money exchange cycle.

Over time, these experiences become reinforced, as the person attracts their vibrational match in having these beliefs. And, unfortunately, money "takes the hit" with their misidentified beliefs, because their money beliefs system is really not about the money.

For example, consider the children's game of telephone—one person whispers to another and they whisper to the next and so on until the last child says out loud the message they heard, only to discover it's completely distorted. There are times when that happens in the money exchange cycle as well—it's no wonder we sometimes repel money on an energetic level and create unconscious paradigms to support our unintentional money sabotage. When we do, this is simply validation of our unclear attraction mechanism as well as a need to heal some part of our being.

As a more personal example, you might have an unconscious money belief that you don't deserve to have money, so earning money is actually a way to punish yourself. If you have this paradigm unconsciously running in your energy body somewhere, you will likely find yourself not ever seeming to have "enough" money. Or you may have a paradigm that drives you to make a lot of money because you feel inherently not worthy, so making money would seem to counter that but, in actuality, having the money reinforces your unworthiness (which is what feeds your personal negative reward system). There's a "payoff" there in some way; surfacing your payoffs is vital to understanding your relationship with money. The consequences of money paradigms can be powerful in determining your relationship with money.

To continue, let's consider some of the most common money models many people hold, maybe even you, which could be unconsciously limiting access to—and programming—your money outcomes.

For a more robust awareness of money models, we need to begin by defining 'paradigm' as a worldview, or lens of perception, through which you see the world and everything in it. A paradigm gives definition to your current reality and, therefore, frames your experience by limiting your fields of awareness through what is familiar to you. You (and every other human!) relate to experiencing something new through what you already know; you can see only what your known reference point allows you to see of any situation in any given moment.

A Set of Limitations
Underscores Your Money

In essence, a paradigm is a set of limitations you bought into as truth and/or created to give structure to your awareness. Paradigms organize, structure and define information; they also potentially limit your ability to see all the possibilities present in whatever you experience based on what you already know—there is simply no frame of reference for what is unknown to you, so seeing (and attempting to understand and organize) new information creates a growth opportunity for you. You have to go beyond your known comfort zone—your existing paradigms—into unfamiliar territory.

When you experience a 'paradigm shift', information you couldn't see before comes into view, providing you with a more expanded foundation for taking in new information and making informed decisions.

Paradigm shifts occur when you decide to take a new or different course of action—your view on the world has to expand to accommodate the new information you need to have toward this new direction. Consider the last time you decided to open a bank account... you probably started seeing more bank ads and billboards, maybe you noticed people using this bank through their checks, and then saw the branch and ATM locations for the bank you were interested in most all over the place. In reality, this is an example of a paradigm shift in action—you started visualizing yourself with an account in this new bank, which sent an image to your current view in your unconscious mind, signaling the need to get more information to support your bank selection decision.

In scientific terms, this is your Reticular Activating System at work. Essentially, the reticular activating system is a network of neurons located in the brain stem that stimulate syncing desynchronized

patterns into relevant meaning. (Lest someo.
tion, please research further on your own to lea.

At any rate, as a consequence of your decision   9
new, you started perceiving more information relevai.
action. Previous to that moment, although the inforn   .s
always available, the information was not determined to be   .por-
tant by your internal filters and was, therefore, screened out of your
awareness. Upon being recognized as important, the new information
becomes available to influence and inform your current thinking and
provide a supportive foundation for you to take action in your chosen
new direction.

We humans have paradigms about pretty much everything
because this is the lens of perception that tells us about our world.
Whenever we experience an energy shift in any area of life, a paradigm shift is sure to follow and/or be noticed. From there, new possibilities present and change is both provoked and empowered. In
other words, your power to create 'lives' in the edges of your paradigms and perception of possibilities.

New paradigms allow you to consider your existing beliefs,
thought patterns, expectations, conditions, projections, assumptions
and limitations to see if they align with your new desired direction.
That is why it is so vital you evaluate your existing paradigms—to
uncover where you have been limiting yourself.

Sustaining Change When You Make It

Any sustainable change process has to consider your paradigms, because they are the patterns of how you have learned to view your world over time. If your lens of perception about the world doesn't change with your new direction / changes, you will still filter what you see and experience according to your previous perceptions (not your new ones.) Paradigms are the effect of old energy; as such, they can be an important clue as to how you have totaled your experience to date and how available you are to see new possibilities.

When your perceptions are running by default unconsciously, you may feel like you are getting inconsistent or even surprising results in what you manifest. That is due to you getting "normal" results, but without consciously realizing what you've asked for in the process.

When what you perceive for what you can have or dream to have is limited (and note that perception is not limited—rather, what you look at or understand is limited), you will likely bump up against constrictive circumstances in attaining it. Whatever you experience in your external world is a reflection of your inner world. As the creator of your experience, what you perceive determines the quality of your life experience.

Since paradigms are the conscious way your linear mind tries to "chunk" energy (by organizing your judgments about the world), your unconscious money paradigms are often the culprits behind your unexpected, unreliable and/or undesired results because they are in stealth mode operating below your level of awareness.

How to Know Your Money Paradigms

Generally speaking, many of your paradigms were imprinted on you before you were able to censor or decide if it was something you wanted to adopt as a worldview. These imprints came from the society around you in your formative years and the people in your world: parents, teachers, church folk, authority figures, friends, etc. (not to mention the stuff you brought with you when you got to this plane of existence!).

All these people loved you and wanted the best for you, and they gave you what they knew to be the best. At the same time, you were also duplicating what they really felt instead of merely doing what they said. Their underlying motivations came through their filters, conditioning, life experience and paradigms. It included their assumptions, their fears and their formula for success—which isn't likely to be yours. However, they gave you the best of what they had at the time. And now the choice and responsibility are yours to locate your paradigms and remove them.

"Unconscious paradigms" (since paradigms can really only exist when we consciously create them) show up when we least expect it. For example, one woman felt she needed to have a degree to have any real value and professional respect in her industry. She worked three jobs, and it took her a decade, but she got it. And when she went into the professional world associated with her degree at long last, nobody really cared—with all her experience, it was assumed she knew her stuff. But her sabotaging paradigm showed itself when she went for promotions, or met new people, because she would always make sure to reference her (lack of) degree.

Her paradigm was a grouping of limitations that fueled her unconscious belief she wasn't valuable without her education, which she actively promoted and which attracted reinforcement of her unconscious need to be worthless, valued only through credentials by her experience with colleagues, who then limited her potential and reduced her credibility. The emphasis she put on her degree actually worked against her but it wasn't about the degree—it was about the power her paradigms assigned to having the degree that made the difference in how people perceived her expertise.

In this case, her "un-conscious" paradigms were sabotaging her success because she had a distorted awareness of her own talent. Her goal was clear, and her talents obvious, but her paradigms prevented her from moving forward. This same dynamic is at play with many, if not most, people in terms of their relationship with money. If a paradigm is in contradiction to current desires, the paradigm has a greater foothold in creating the experience because it is harnessing the power of pre-set structures (symbolizing order and security—we humans have a strong paradigm to be safe). So the paradigm has more power in determining outcomes vs. the current desire, even if powered by education and tangible action. (The exception would be when the 'pay-off' rewards the existing but unknown paradigm.)

Another common belief is that money is available only in short supply; however, the government printing and minting of money is in continuous operation, not to mention all the "digital" money being exchanged right now between bank accounts all over the world. Beyond that, money isn't actually related to physical money... the physical money is just an effect of money energy. Money energy is what creates the physical means to reference money energy. So money is really not in short supply; instead, it is the "gunk" (your paradigms) in the way to your own money access that makes it seem like money is limited.

Let's try a few exercises to tease your money paradigms out of your unconscious mind. Before we begin, know this kind of illumination can initiate an energy shift and a paradigm change process. Where there is light, there cannot be darkness, so simply identifying contradictory or negative money paradigms begins the release process (because you'll move toward your proverbial light).

Remember paradigms are simply a conscious grouping of limitations, so letting those go and opening up to new perceptions can create exponential shifts in your overall life experience (not related to just money). To surface your unconscious paradigms through this kind of work makes them conscious and accessible to you.

While you have paradigms about every life area, we are most interested in the ones that relate to you and your money. That said, with a little modification, you can use these exercises to better understand your paradigms in other life areas as well.

As you go, there will be some suggestions on how to handle the paradigms you don't want anymore (which creates space for new incoming energy).

Exercise 1: Money Map

In the center of a large piece of clean paper, write the word 'Money' in the center. Take a moment to consider everything that word represents to you… with each insight, write it on the paper and draw a line to it from that central word (it will eventually look like spokes on a wheel). Ask yourself what money represents for you, what sources you currently have for money, how do you feel about having / not having money, how you spend your money, what are the threads of your money over your lifetime… and if you come across any concepts that relate to the secondary word, draw the lines from that instead of the central word.

As a result of this exercise, you may discover how you relate to money, uncover hidden beliefs about money, or use words you wouldn't expect to describe money. These are all clues to the money paradigms underlying your conscious mind and which could be tripping you up in your present-day relationship with money. The key is to know none of them are true—they are just misidentified and misapplied concepts that are, or have become, limiting to you and your money.

Exercise 2: Childhood Beliefs

Write out the most common statements you remember hearing as a child about money. This list could include some of the following statements.

"Money doesn't grow on trees."
"Money is the root of all evil."
"There's never enough money."
"We can't afford that."
"You have to work hard (sacrifice) for money."
"You're too young to decide what you want."
"Ask your father for your allowance."

What other beliefs did you hear and imprint as a child that could be affecting your money now?

Notice how each statement is, or could be, true and how each statement is, or could be, false. By changing your point of view, you can change the truth or falseness of these beliefs. Change how you define the words and you can manipulate the meaning for each statement—this is proof that beliefs can be simply misidentifications or misapplied concepts in your own mind.

Consider what the outcomes of those paradigms on your list might be... for example, if as a youngster, your father was the one with the money, do you expect men to give you money? Is there a virtual authority figure between you and your money? Is there something you need to do before you can have the money that has been earmarked for you? The responses you have to these types of questions can be very insightful about your money paradigms.

Take a moment to consider how these beliefs feel in your body—do you feel good or do you feel drained? Here is the catch: both of these are potential hooks to control you and limit your choices, and that includes the "good" ones. Look at both states of your emotional response as a clue on how to actively change your relationship with money.

Exercise 3: Words and Phrases of Money

Draw a line down the center of a piece of paper. On the left side, write out the words that you use and associate with money (for example, greenbacks, dollars, paper, coin, etc.). On the right side, write out the phrases you use to talk about money (for example, I always need money, I never have enough money, I want to make more money, I deserve to be wealthy, etc.).

Once your lists feel complete, read them out loud. Notice how you feel with each word or phrase you read out loud verbally and what comes up for you as you pay attention to both the vibration of the word as you say it and how your body responds to it.

There is nothing "good" or "bad" here… this is simply a way for you to understand your own money language. You will either discover a message about how to use money words more effectively, or a limitation in how you are relating with money. In either case, this is valuable information! Give consideration to how you can be more expansive in your money language, as that will affect your overall relationship with money.

Exercise 4: Your Money Story

This is a simple writing exercise that can reveal a lot about your money paradigms. On a clean piece of paper, write the description of your ideal house. Include specific references to how you feel living in it, how comfortable it is to live in, how the rooms are laid out, the décor, how spacious or intimate it feels, your favorite rooms—really bring your dream home to life in your words. Remember this is about what you want to experience with your home, not what is actually happening now or where you are currently living. And it is not about whether you can, or even should, ever have it—this is about putting your dreams on paper. (At this point, you are encouraged to actually do the exercise before reading the next section on how to apply the teaching to what you have written.)

Once you have completed the writing exercise, read your short story out loud to yourself (or a trusted friend). As you do, replace the words 'home', 'house' or 'space' with the word 'money', and see how the story changes. As you relate to your ideal home is likely to be close to how you relate to your money. This exercise will likely reveal to you how you believe your life would be different with money, where you are experiencing lack in your dreams about money, and how open you are to new possibilities with money.

A secondary benefit to this exercise is that your conscious mind will start to create this ideal home in reality because you have engaged the power of energy and your unconscious mind in the manifestation process—you are bringing a lot of power to what's being created. So, as you write it with conviction, you are planting seeds of growth toward your ideal living space. The theory is the same as the above example with choosing a new bank; you have now engaged your conscious and unconscious mind into helping create the circumstances that you desire.

Exercise Summary:

Now that you have some insights as to your personal money paradigms, take some time to assimilate them into a cohesive list. Of course, they are already shifting because they are now known. To help them release even faster, engage your linear mind in a dialogue about each of them. One at a time, ask yourself the following three questions.

Is this true? (If you get YES, you are stuck—time to revisit what gives you a sting, ping, or "charge" for clues on what to shift.)

Is this working for me? (As in, do you want to keep this as a truth?)

What do I need to do to release and heal this issue?

Wait to get your answers, and, based on what comes up for you, note the actions which are delivered to you through your wisdom. Of course, you may not be able to do what is needed immediately, but you can set and schedule your intentions to facilitate positive momentum in perceiving new information and shifting these 'old' paradigms.

The Effects of Existing Money Paradigms

It is largely a lack of awareness about your money patterns and paradigms that will distort, control, limit or even block incoming money and/or money messages.

As an example, if you owe someone a large sum of money, and you have resentment about that debt for some reason, you may unconsciously be keeping yourself in poverty to avoid repaying the debt. Or if you have energetically bound having a significant other relationship with making money, that will drive you to either make a lot of money or to not have enough money, depending on your view of relationship. It is human nature to keep doing what's familiar, even if it's hurtful or dysfunctional, simply because it's comfortable on some level.

By the by, this is not about giving yourself an excuse to beat yourself up over whatever you discover… there is no judgment about what is right or wrong, or if you are a good person or not. That has nothing to do with this kind of self-inquiry. All the insights you gain are saying is that routine is preferable to chaos, and dysfunctional familiarity is likely to win over uncomfortable growth. Where it becomes challenging is when you do not know what your patterns are, so you don't know what you need to change to get new results.

Your money paradigms filter what comes into your life through the 'tint' of its lens. So, if you are angry and jealous that someone else is more financially successful than you, that energy will filter everything you see in relation to money through anger and jealousy. It will become more pervasive over time, and you will see others through that same filter. The energy will build and you will likely find more substantiation of why you should have anger and jealousy through more examples that show up for you as that energy colors everything that comes into your life experience. You are attracting that which you are as evidenced by how you are experiencing money.

If one of your 'unconscious' paradigms is that you need to struggle to have money, or need to use force and energy to get money, you will continue to find yourself in situations which facilitate that exact thing in happening—you will have to fight for your money somehow. In this case, your limiting belief is conditioning the circumstances around you to support what your self-talk and imprinted patterns are internally reinforcing as your expected experience. By being unconscious to it, you will consciously be upset and confused as to why that's happening—which adds more negative energy (or raw power / fuel) to the need to fight. And so you fight harder…

Duplicated Money Paradigms You Inherited

As already mentioned, you duplicated a lot of these money paradigms from your parents, authority figures, and teachers (among others) before you knew what you were doing. In fact, each of those people duplicated their money paradigms from the people in their world, and those people from the people in their world before that. Ostensibly, many of the paradigms you hold true were likely developed hundreds of years ago, passed down through the ages without question, without logical relevance and which do not support your awareness. Lots of people believe and create what they think they do not want, simply because they are running off default, "ancestral" duplicated patterns.

As an example, a common paradigm that constricts new money messages is that you have not worked hard enough to have earned it. What follows is a wildly speculative statement on our part, but this particular belief seems to have originated from historical institutions that needed to find a way to control the masses (corporate dictators, religious institutions and the like). If someone is kept humble, they are less likely to upset the social order of whatever system in which they are a part. In modern living, this is still very much in play (with government systems, politics, religious institutions and more), and there are powerful fears that keep people locked in place ("golden handcuffs" of a nice salary, not knowing how to strike out on their own, losing health insurance, etc.).

Another way to see where your money paradigms are blocking incoming money energy is to evaluate whether you have sufficient funds to do what you want when you want. It can be painful to not have the money to do what you want, so you might change what you want to something smaller and sub-standard, or focus on being grateful for what you have and not asking for more in an attempt to keep you from experiencing the pain of the limitation which is not allowing you to have more. If you do not have the funds you want when you want them, there's a good chance something is distorting or blocking your incoming money messages.

Caveat: there is something beneficial about being grateful for what you have now because, in that gratitude, you are empowering yourself to create more of what you want. So yes—be grateful! AND do not let that stop you from asking for more of what you want.

Common Money Saboteurs

Here is a list of some of the more common saboteurs that could be tripping you up.

- You have misidentified, or misapplied, what attracting, creating, making, or having money means.
- You undervalue or minimize the importance of money in your life.
- You associate money with negative connotations, relationships, or results.
- You rely on others to give you your money messages (accountant, teacher, parent, spouse, etc.).
- You harbor a pain, resentment or directed challenge that is more painful than the benefit of attracting, creating, making, or having money.
- You hold on to your money instead of allowing it to freely circulate and create miracles.
- You feel like you are not perfect enough on some level to warrant attracting, creating, making, or having money.
- Your connection to Source (whatever that means to you) for your money messages is minimal or non-existent, or, when you do get your money messages, you don't definitively know what you know about them.
- You do not see your money messages, potential or opportunities in the world around you.
- You have misidentified that your financial state is a reflection of your success and ability to handle what life brings you.
- You ask for 'just enough' to pay the bills, without thinking or dreaming bigger.

- You make financial decisions based on external circumstances, others' opinion, or fear.
- You have gotten comfortable with your financial status and do not proactively cultivate a bigger relationship with money in knowledge or action.
- You do not trust you can have a healthy relationship with bigger money now.

If any of these seem like you, there is a saboteur distorting your relationship with money. In each case, you can now see you could be experiencing a variety of negative consequences when it is present on any level.

The good news is it's easier to clear a known saboteur than to be controlled by an unknown one. Think of it as a direct message on where you can begin healing your relationship with money.

That means congratulations are in order—you are no longer hiding your personal way to wealth from yourself!

Handling Your Money Saboteurs and Unwanted Paradigms

One of the most amazing discoveries you might have made by now is that, by itself, money has energy. If it has no energy, it has not been created yet; if it is not money, then it is something else—simply paper with symbols on it. Until it is energized to have money energy, it does not have the value of money. Once it is "created" into money, it has the energy of money and is a symbol of wealth and a measure of value exchanged (which is a reflection of the money user).

The same applies to digital money—an online account could be a paper account to practice trading stocks but becomes a money account when energized with money by the user in the form of a deposit of funds to back the account.

Before getting into the language of money, it makes sense to give you some guidelines and tools by which to shift your relationship with money and clear the undesirable energy blocks in your way for all the wealth you desire.

To begin at the beginning, you MUST claim the results with which you are living right now. This goes beyond gratitude to personal accountability.

Your outer world is an expression of your inner world, and where you are now is the result of the choices, decisions and commitments you have made previously (whether consciously or unconsciously). It is ONLY by claiming your results that you can own your power to manifest and, therefore, empower yourself to create new results in your future.

To supercharge stepping into your power by claiming where you are, you can use your voice. Your voice is the vibration of your essence so, when you speak out loud, you are expressing your power into the Universe. You can use your voice to express gratitude, which acknowledges the gifts in where you are, and you can express your gratitude in advance of what is coming (which sets intention in motion).

Give yourself credit for the good job you have done already with the positives in your life and business, which gives a natural incentive to create your future consciously. You can speak daily affirmations, clearing statements and declarations of your ability to generate results. In any way you use your voice, you are using your vibration to create; as with anything, be conscious of how you are using that power in every moment. Add extra power to your vocal vibration energy by matching the energy of the word with the energy you feel... for example, say 'happy' and feel happy vs. saying 'happy' and feeling sad.

Negative Mental
Voices Aren't Real

Focus on the potential solutions as they present and follow where your contemplations and intuitive wisdom lead you. It isn't actually important you resolve the situation; more important is that you pay attention to what may result from the process of exploring it without attachment to what 'was' previously or an outcome you want to have now. By being with the flow of the energy, you are exploring something important to how you are relating with the world (and, in particular, money) without making it conditional on where you've been or where you are going—that allows a new measure of freedom for true understanding from your soul.

Remember the negative self-talk isn't 'you'; it is an old memory / message expressing itself without a direct reflection of your current truth.

So why does negative self-talk show up? Because we humans have a part of our brain that is ancient and is the source of primary survival energy: the amygdala. The amygdala focuses on patterns and, when there is something too far out of your comfort zone, it lets you know about a possible threat. It is a primitive warning system. However, you do have the ability to take action based on what you decide in the moment.

These 'old' messages have a biological base that can kick off your survival fears but, over time, they become a habitual pattern of relating to your world from a negative viewpoint. It becomes an ingrained way of perceiving your world, with the information for your survival being designated to be of greater importance than is 'right' for you. Survival trumps abundance. (Remember Maslow's Hierarchy of Needs?)

Naturally, you are seeking as much information as you can get throughout your day. However, these particular negative self-talk messages no longer serve a positive purpose because they are now irrelevant and not helpful in owning your power. They are fear- and survival-based vs. being self-actualization and power-based.

Think of negative self-talk as a painting created by an artist... just because the painting exists does not mean it is the only thing the artist can create; the artist is not limited in expression by creating a painting. Likewise, your self-talk is not an indicator that it is your only language of expression to yourself. You are unlimited in choosing how you want to talk to yourself; negative self-talk is a re-tread of old self-judgments, projections, and proclamations. Your "painting" is not a permanent statement of your internal language but, instead, is an effect of how you have been unconscious in how you treat yourself. The good news is you can choose a new way of expressing yourself to yourself by being conscious. You are not limited in your options; instead, it is your view that you are limited which makes it so.

So, these self-talk survival mechanism messages, once meant to protect you, have become negative self-talk by broadcasting a message based on information that is not relevant to you. They are taking up mind-space, sabotaging your progress and actually eroding your ability to proactively create what you want and access the abundance around you in every moment. You can know this by how you feel when they are playing in your mind—if you listen to them and you don't feel good or you feel 'attached' to them or you can't understand a clear way to use that information, these are the real saboteurs to your success.

Use Your Amygdala's
Ability to Sense Info

All that said, there IS a way you can use your amygdala's ability to sense information. We know its job is to find all the ways you are not safe, but the current reality is you ARE safe—there are no more saber-toothed tigers waiting to eat you. So the information your amygdala is getting is correct, but it is pointed toward 'reading' information for you from the wrong place. Think of how powerful it would be to direct this hard-wired survival mechanism toward you what will support you in thriving financially.

As an example, think about what your amygdala is doing from a traditional viewpoint by considering a lake dam. If you are standing on the "dry" side, looking up at the dam wall, your amygdala is assessing where the leaks are, where the potential cracks and weaknesses could be, and what action you need to take to protect yourself from harm if the dam breaks. There is a lot of force and energy holding that dam in place.

However, if you were on the other side of the dam, where all the stored water is being held, you would experience that the water needs to get through or over the dam in order to flow. The 'lake' side of the dam perceives the dam as a limitation. What if you were to use your amygdala from this side of the dam to understand where the areas of greatest flow might be attained?

What if you were to find the 'weaknesses' in the wall that would actually create more flow in your life?

In the same way, you can theoretically point your amygdala to assessing where the weaknesses or cracks are in creating greater flow in your life. Where could you be accessing even more information or abundance through key connections that you have actually been blocking as a preventive measure from the 'other' side?

By educating yourself on the possibilities from a different vantage point, you are moving the antenna of your reception to getting new information that helps create more possibility and abundant flow in your life. You can continue that educational process by following through on where your curiosity is led; fill yourself with positive information through reading, classes, and workshops, and, most importantly, your own connection with Source energy. Just as additional nutrients will help any living thing to grow, educating yourself on the information you receive is vital to expanding your capacity to receive more abundance in every way.

One other important aspect about adding to your ability to handle undesirable paradigms effectively is to have supportive, like-spirited people in your world. We humans are meant to be social, and community is an important aspect of feeling like we have a place to 'belong', that we are understood, and that we have back-up for both the tough spots and the celebrations.

The caveat to this concept, however, is something that may actually seem counter-productive. That is, when you use community to 'self-verify', as in, when you don't use this as a measure of the energy you are presenting outwardly but, instead, seek others to reflect back to the beliefs you already have about yourself, it is a disservice to yourself (not to mention your tribe).

Your Community Reflects Your Greater Truths

Your chosen community needs to be a place where you can receive feedback on who you are showing up to be and, ideally, is a positive sounding board for you. (By the way, "positive" in this sense does not necessarily mean easy, comfortable or what you want to hear... "positive" is the highest vibration that will help you to grow in the most powerful, supported way possible.)

Your tribe holds a lot of generative power for you, but it can also, by definition, be controlling. In order to be a good member of any community, you need to know its rules, ethics, behavior expectations and have loyalty towards it and its members. You must choose a community that supports you as an individual, even as you participate within it.

Once you have found such a community within which to relate and be all of who you are, this is where you can express your saboteurs to get an outside perspective.

According to Einstein, the same energy that created a problem cannot solve it so, to understand your saboteurs better, it can be helpful to get additional perspective from people who know and/or understand you (or who are willing to explore with you).

In any case, by paying attention to your saboteurs and being more aware of your paradigms, you give yourself the power to choose their ability to affect your life and wealth. No longer will your decisions be made by things that are not you, whether they are negative self-talk gremlins, echoes from a past situation, projected fears, or outdated paradigms. You are in charge of the receipt and interpretation of your messages as they relate to who you are now.

The Language of Wealth Patterns and Money Messages

Money Is a Choice

Money, and having plenty of it, is simply a choice. Many people (including you) have misidentified that money is something other than what it is, or it has a meaning different than what it means. It is an energy, just like a house is an energy. There is an energy associated with having a house that manifests in the outer world; the different 'flavors' of energy determine what kind of house you live in (how big it is, where it's located, whether you own it, etc.). The house is a physical symbol of your relationship to 'house' energy, just like the amount of money you access is a symbol of your clear connection to money.

As you grow in understanding both your wealth patterns and your money messages, you give yourself the opportunity to experience whatever you choose in terms of your wealth experience, with a greater chance for doing it consistently.

Your Wealth Patterns

By definition, a pattern is an action or behavior that happens repetitively and, over time, becomes a habitual way, or default script, of thinking of doing something. Your wealth patterns are the habitual ways you have of thinking of and/or relating to money in your life. In this section, we will consider how your wealth patterns are showing up currently to help you determine whether they are what you consciously want in your life.

As humans, it is our natural proclivity to try to assign patterns to our world in an attempt to create security through systems. We assign meaning based on what we think / feel and then assimilate it as a truth from that point forward. However, when those patterns become default by rote, and we are not happy with the results we are getting, it is time to revisit the source of those patterns. Your wealth patterns (both in thoughts and behavior) include anything about your relationship with money, such as: how you spend, invest, save, pay out, shop with, receive, manifest and more.

Non-Supportive Patterns for Wealth

There are certain wealth patterns that people who do not have a wealthy relationship with money typically experience in their minds. Such individuals will find the following types of thoughts in their mind.

> I'll never be wealthy ⇨ I don't know how to get wealthy ⇨ Other people know more than me how to get / be wealthy ⇨ I'm not good with numbers ⇨ I don't deserve to be rich ⇨ I don't look like a wealthy

person ⇨ I'm not from a rich family / my parents
weren't rich ⇨ I don't have the right background to be
wealthy ⇨ Wealthy people are glamorous and I'm not
⇨ I really wouldn't know what to do with a lot of
money ⇨ I don't know how to invest money ⇨ I don't
have the right job / business to get rich ⇨ I don't have
the right skills / abilities to become rich ⇨ I have good
reasons that I haven't been able to save money (and it's
unlikely those will ever change) ⇨ The economy
makes it hard for me to get rich ⇨ Wealthy people are
mean / stingy / unethical / ruthless / ungrateful ⇨
I'm not smart enough to be rich ⇨ It's not my fault that
I'm in financial struggle ⇨ I'm in so much debt that I
can never be rich ⇨ And more...

Do you recognize yourself in any of these wealth thought patterns? If you felt a sting, a ping, or a 'charge' when reading any of those, there is an unhealthy wealth pattern lurking in your mind somewhere. (Kudos on finding it...) ;+)

Supportive Patterns for Wealth

In contrast, let's consider some wealth thought patterns that financially successful people have as a part of their mindset. See if you see yourself in any of the following statements.

I deserve to have money / be wealthy ⇨ I know I have
what it takes to be rich ⇨ I have confidence in my
skills, talents and abilities ⇨ I believe in myself and my
awareness in making decisions ⇨ I don't need
anybody else's thoughts, opinions or approval ⇨ I
know even my stretch goals are attainable (with
enough time) ⇨ I am compelled to do what I do

because I am aligned with my purpose in being ⇨ I
know I can do anything I want to do / be / have ⇨ If
other people have been rich, I can do it too (and if they
haven't, I can figure it out!) ⇨ I have everything I need
to succeed at whatever I want ⇨ I know that taking
risks is important to go beyond my comfort zone and
trust my resilience in handling whatever happens ⇨
It's important for me to have access to people who can
help me (mentor, coach, guide, teacher, etc.) and it is an
investment in myself for me to work with them ⇨ I am
in charge of my future and willing to accept that
responsibility in every way ⇨ And more...

Can you feel the difference in the thought energy between people who are not wealthy and those who are likely to be wealthy? Can you relate with the second set of thoughts on any level? Maybe you find that you have a reaction or resistance to some of these thoughts, which is a big clue as to patterns running at some level of your being and which may not be serving you. Or maybe you find these typical of your current thoughts now... if yes, ask yourself if these are representative of your consistent wealth thoughts (which would be ideally supportive for you and would make a vibrational match with money).

In any case, these thought patterns are affecting your relationship with wealth; by cultivating your awareness, you are giving yourself the ability to be at choice. By having a conscious presence to the thoughts that are creating your actions and, therefore, results, you are cultivating a healthier relationship with money.

Since the thoughts of each type of person have a real-world, physical effect on choices and behaviors, let's consider some of the contrasting behaviors between people who are not—and are—financially wealthy.

Common Behaviors of People Who Are Not Wealthy

Following are typical or common behaviors of people who do not have a wealthy relationship with money.

Live from paycheck to paycheck ⇨ Pay themselves last ⇨ Rely on others opinions, direction, example or expertise to make financial decisions ⇨ Listen to money "guru-types" ⇨ Give into "instant gratification" strategies for wealth ⇨ Think they'll feel better in the moment by giving into immediate gratification purchases (whether they can pay for it or not at the time) ⇨ Think they have to "keep up" with their friends, colleagues and neighbors for appearances and belongings ⇨ "Chase" money / quick cash ⇨ Are oblivious to cash flow drains ⇨ Are "victim" to their money (which puts their money, or lack of it, in charge of decisions) ⇨ See the short-term but minimize or negate long-term views of their money ⇨ Spend more than they earn ⇨ Think tomorrow will be a "better day" ⇨ Put off taking action for their financial wellness ⇨ Are bargain-shoppers and coupon-users ⇨ Don't budget their money or understand where it's going ⇨ Don't diversify their income / revenue streams ⇨ Rely on credit regularly ⇨ And more…

Common Behaviors of Wealthy People

Now let's look at the behaviors of people who have positive wealth thought patterns and how that manifests tangibly through their choices and actions:

Look for opportunities to create / attract / access / have money ⇨ Understand the concept of opportunity cost ⇨ Seek value vs. "brand" names ⇨ Know the value of time ⇨ Pay themselves first ⇨ Don't use credit or credit cards without significant reason (rarely) ⇨ Have a financial plan and reserves available ⇨ Diversify their income / revenue / investments ⇨ Exhibit financial resilience through tough times ⇨ Know where their money is coming from and going to ⇨ Take action in the 'now' ⇨ Learn about money and financial management concepts / strategies ⇨ Consider their return on any investment (of money, but time / energy / resources as well) ⇨ Use appropriate discipline in their relationship with money ⇨ And more...

Which type of behaviors speaks to your currently active relationship with money? If you are in the latter group, you are doing great—keep going! And if you are in the former, you are doing great—now get going! ;+)

In all seriousness, you are now at choice because you have a better understanding of your wealth patterns. You cannot unlearn what you now know. If your money patterns are not what you want, knowing that is the greatest gift which can potentially change the rest of your life. By understanding your wealth patterns, you have a place to begin in predicting your own behavior in advance AND in revealing your hidden money beliefs.

If the question in your head is "how do rich people get rich?", this is the time to find out... through your own experience!

Understand Your Money Messages

By this point, you are starting to get a good idea of your money messages based on the exercises in this book as well as by increasing your awareness of your triggers and wealth patterns. At this point, the next step is to become aware of how your money messages are presenting, understanding what they are telling you, and what to do with them.

Types of Money Messages

As with any other message, your money messages may show up by using a number of different "languages". Generally speaking, if you are not fluent in one language, the message will show up in another until you get it. Or, you may find repetition of the message in the same language or multiple languages until you get it. A good rule of thumb is: when you get something twice, write it down—when you get a message three times, decide what you're going to do with it because it's definitely meant for you.

Here are three ways you might receive your money messages (although keep in mind that you may have a different language than the ones listed here).

Visual Money Messages

Visual money messages are delivered via your eyesight, either physically or psychically. This means you might see a money message in a billboard, advertisement, magazine, newspaper, street sign… anything with a place for messages. It may come through as words, but also, know that it can come to you through an image or picture. Messages often speak through pictures because images access a deeper part of our brain than the linear mind, which then organizes according to words. This is the language of psychic visuals, which may come through sudden insights or dreams.

For example, one of my clients wanted to know which business opportunity to pursue. In thinking about it, he asked to see a sign so he would know that was the right direction. He asked to see an angel to confirm his thought process. He let that idea go and went about his day. Naturally, he explored both opportunities in some way—talking about them, doing research, meeting people who could help, etc. He didn't think about the angel, until driving home from meeting someone who was interested in one of the ideas. In front of him while driving was a bus—with a big billboard on the backend with an angel on it! That was how he knew that was his best opportunity which, in time, proved to be true.

Audio Money Messages

Just as with the visual messages, audio messages may show up through the vibration of sound, including someone talking to you, overhearing someone else's conversation, a radio / tv show, an internet radio interview, or some other "external" world way. You may also hear a voice or words in your head, pick up something from a dream, or hear a faint whisper that echoes after something else happens (you meet someone, you watch a movie, etc.).

One of my clients, a real estate agent, kept hearing the word "roses" in her mind. She had no idea why. After a couple of weeks, she decided to go to the local do-it-yourself supply store and, spontaneously, went to see the gardening section and look for roses. When she did, there was someone else looking at them too. They struck up a conversation. It turned out that her conversation partner had a home he was looking to sell and was increasing the curb appeal by planting roses—and he needed an agent.

Body Money Messages

Body messages occur when you receive your money insights through your body. For example, there are some classic body messages: your palm itches when money is coming in, your handshakes when you write a check you're not sure will clear, you sweat when thinking about going to your tax accountant or your stomach gets upset when balancing your checkbook. You will also feel a surge of adrenalin when you get an unexpected windfall or give yourself permission to go shopping. Think of your body as a giant antenna to help you bring in your money messages.

Symbology of Money

One last point... when your money messages are coming in, it is highly likely they will use symbols to make their point.

That is, it is not always the case that money will show up in the form of cash but, instead, you may get images of lots of horses running toward the barn (which are opportunities heading toward a safe, nourishing environment that is waiting for them), or frogs (a traditional Feng Shui symbol of prosperity) or something that personally represents wealth or money for you.

In fact, it is the personal symbols which hold the most power in any money message; if you have a personal symbol (your wallet) and a universal symbol (your stove—because when you have something to cook on your stove, you are wealthy) in the same message, pay particular attention to the personal symbol and what it's telling you.

One man always sees a butterfly in some form when he is about to receive money; he has found that he will get an unexpected check, a new client or somehow find money within 24 hours of seeing a butterfly. When pressed to give details, he said he's seen butterflies in the clouds, on an advertisement, on a postcard... he's even seen one formed in the side of a mountain by the crevices and shadows. However his butterfly shows up, it always foretells money for him.

Another woman has discovered her symbols of money to include some sort of travel vehicle. On three different occasions, she dreamt of an airplane, a hot air balloon and a race car and, within the next three weeks of her dreams, she received money from unexpected sources.

The Universe is always talking to you and giving you messages about your money. Another example of this is a woman who had a lawsuit pending for more than three years for an injury she sustained to her foot while on the corporation's property. In working with the

Feng Shui of her property, I determined her recently installed corkscrew staircase was in the area of her home related to the foot; when she adjusted her staircase using a Feng Shui cure and ritual, her case settled (to her benefit) within the next month. And her physician advised that her foot was healing at a faster rate than previously predicted; she recovered completely soon after. This is a good example of the relationship between your internal and external worlds, as well as the power of stuck energy that, once released, provides for optimal flow in multiple life areas.

One more way to ascertain the symbology of your money is to look at your 'money mirrors'. Just like a dressing mirror, where you see yourself in the reflection, you can see your relationship with money in the mirrors around you in your life and environment. As already mentioned, what's "in here" is what's "out there", so you can use the external markers of your world to help you understand what is happening for you internally.

Your money mirrors may include the people in your world, so consider who you are relating with and then consider how you see them relating to their money. Chances are you have some of the same qualities or characteristics about money as the people who are closest to you in your world. If you have a group of friends who are cavalier about money and splurge with their purchases, that may be a part of the social code you ascribe to by being a part of that "tribe" because of the shared expected, normalized behavior of treating money casually.

Another money mirror is your physical environment. The space(s) in which you live and work need to support you in a way that is aligned with your energy. You must feel comfortable, supported, and have positive energy flow in and around you. It is important you are able to function without distraction, that everything is in clean, working order and that you have space to grow. If your environment is restrictive, dirty, has broken aspects, is unsafe or does not reflect your personality and needs, it is a money mirror that shows some active core money beliefs for you.

Yet another money mirror is how you handle social situations. When you are out, whether with friends or alone, how do you spend your money? What is important here is what motivates you to spend your money... do you purchase based on impulse or with deliberate awareness? Do you purchase things that are "first-class" or just "filler"? Do you order from the menu based on price or based on what you really want? Notice your social / purchasing mirrors to gain insight into your own money messages.

Receiving Your Money Messages

You can ask for money messages to come in as an answer to a specific question, or to get a general direction on the state of your finances, or to receive next action steps on how to 'heal' your relationship with money. By simply asking for insight, you are opening the portal for your own money messages to show up.

By focusing your energies this way, and paying attention to what comes in, you are choosing abundant thoughts. Contrary to what you might think, it is not important whether you believe this will work for you or not; instead, when you are open to receiving your messages, they will show up. This type of consciousness initiates a whole new level of connection with your money messages.

When you get your money messages, whatever way they present, pay attention to how you feel about them. Should you find you have resistance or a reaction (whether positive or negative), you are experiencing some stored energy you can channel in a generative way toward a wealthier relationship with money.

For example, if the money message you receive is you have to wait for your ship to come in, feel your response to that. If you are upset, frustrated or even angry about having to wait, you have attached some meaning somewhere about why you can't have it now or that you aren't enough somehow to have earned it or hold some other (unconscious) belief that is wreaking havoc with your connection to wealth.

On the other hand, when you get that message and celebrate your money is on its way, your perception will help make that happen more easily. (Note: this is also an obvious example of your perception 'filter' coloring or translating the message through what is already in your vibrational energy field.)

Therefore, a money message is actually a neutral energy, neither positive nor negative until you make it have meaning. Your Source, or universal energy, generally delivers whatever you need to get to your next best level as an opportunity, not a punishment (although there may be times when it's challenging to do whatever is needed to follow through on what you've learned). Things happen for you, not to you, when you can see life with a metaphysical lens.

Following are some common money messages to use as a gauge in determining your own 'lens' of perception. Read the following money messages and feel how each one (and their opposite) feels in your body to give you an idea of your body sensations in "reading" your money messages.

I deserve / don't deserve to have more money.

I do / do not deserve to enjoy the money I have.

More money will / will not make my life better.

There will never be enough money.

Money is / isn't important.

I can / cannot afford anything I want.

It's time / not time for me to spend money on me.

By paying attention to your response to the above money messages, you are developing your awareness. Now you know what each message feels like in your body. Remember, wherever you felt a sting, ping or 'charge', there is likely some stuck energy that needs to be released.

One often recommended technique is to use money mantras as pre-determined money messages to activate in your life through repetition what you want to experience in your physical world. Simply hold the money mantras in your mind (one or all, either the following or your own) and, if it feels right, say them out loud verbally at the same time.

Following are some money mantras for you to play with and see how they feel for you.

> I expect miracles around money every day.

> Every dollar (pound, yen, etc.) I circulate brings me at least three back.

> I have more than enough money to pay for all my wants, needs and desires.

The key is to 'feel' your belief behind these statements to activate their money message qualities. If you do not have an emotional engagement with the statement, it obviously does not have the same level of ability to be an intentional, powerful money message for you.

Another technique to 'tease' your money messages out into the open is to ask yourself extreme questions about money. For example, ask yourself "is it ok for me to have more money than I need?, " is it ok for me to have a million dollars today?", then "is it ok for me to have ten million dollars right now?".

Escalating the questions you ask will exacerbate the feeling in your body, trigger an emotional response and activate your linear mind with thoughts about those questions and how to answer them. Pay attention to what shows up as you get creative and ask yourself extreme money questions… and receive your money messages.

Trust and Money: The Dance for Your Abundance

If you do not trust you will have enough money to meet your wants and needs, or that you will have no way to generate / attract / attain it, you are essentially stating you don't trust yourself nor the Universe. How would you feel if someone you considered a friend were to tell you they did not trust you to be there for them? It does not feel good… and that is the message you are giving to yourself AND the Universe on a regular basis when you are in doubt, fear, worry or scarcity around money. (Luckily, Source does not take it personally; unfortunately, you do.)

Generally speaking, you are where you are now because you've always had the money you needed to get to where you are (that's by definition—otherwise, you wouldn't be where you are now, right?). That is not to say it has been easy, or planned for, or even that it happened with any degree of grace… but you made it to where you are now. On some level, you were cared for even when you were not so sure about it.

Another way to look at this is to consider how you have allocated the money you did have, because you will likely see it wasn't the money but your choice as to how to spend it which demonstrated your level of trust with it.

For example, when you know you really need to see a chiropractor but never really get to it for perceived financial reasons, but you find a way to go to movies or get a haircut (or any other myriad of ways to spend money), the question wasn't the lack of money—it was how you chose to spend it. And if you DID use it to pay for something for your self-care, it's likely you found a way to pay for the 'wants' too.

The Universe, or Source, always provides for you and rewards the degree of your alignment with money energy.

To the degree you trust money to be there for you and clear the path for it to find you is to the degree you are aligned with it and to which it becomes available. This is not a qualitative relationship where you have to be a good person to have money; rather, by trusting you are provided for, by receiving, understanding and acting on your money messages and by being conscious of your relationship with money, you are aligning yourself with the energy of money.

And may you have plenty of it.

The Eight Money Lies for Which No One Has Answers

About Gurus and Gunk

The purpose of this section is to explore the money lies people do not talk about, that do not have answers by conventional method and which are preventing people from enjoying more money in their lives. It exposes the half-truths that, taken individually, work against reality.

With the economy, media hype and people's attention being on the negative about money, there is a lot of information circulating about wealth and money. Most of it is not particularly helpful, nor is it designed to be... even the self-proclaimed wealth gurus teaching about money do not take on the hidden issues, which are usually a lot harder than people want to know. And when people do not want to know it, the gurus lose money by talking about it, so they don't— there is a disincentive to them to go too far into these topics.

That doesn't even consider the fact that most gurus don't know how to solve money issues, which means their wealth-building models don't work unless you happen to be one of the special few who don't have the hidden blocks their models depend on you not having (or their model does work—only it's to build their personal wealth instead of yours!).

As with any true recovery process, you have to look at the 'gunky' stuff in order for the truth to be revealed.

On the one hand, it is undesirable to want to look at the mucky, shadowy, distasteful things that could be painful. However, on the other hand, by exploring exactly those things, they are seen, you are at choice with them (instead of letting them control you unconsciously as a default program), and they lose their power as you begin to accept and work with them.

Through illuminating the following eight money lies that really have not been—until now—talked about openly, you could clear (and even heal) some core aspects of your relationship with money. This could help you experience a whole new way of being in the world—things flow easier, you attract and enjoy more abundance in all ways, and you feel deeply satisfied and more with your life.

Altogether, this book is intended to set in motion your exploration of the 'gunky' stuff, which is potentially and subversively distorting your relationship with money. So get comfortable and notice which (if not all) of the following eight money lies could be playing a role in your life up until now.

Money Is…

Money is a lot of things—the measure of success or failure, the ability and security to provide for self and family, the currency to create future, and more. It is tied to professional career, goal achievement and sense of personal and professional identity. Money means being able to go out and buy what you want when you want it—and not having money means being denied what you want.

Not having money is also a powerful state that can dictate how you live your life. It forces you to live according to priorities that keep you small, including working at a job where someone else determines not only your value but your standard of living by paying you what they think you and your time are worth.

Money is a status symbol. Money is power. And money is generally accepted as a social norm in that it does not grow on trees—you have to work hard to get it, and you cannot just buy whatever you want willy-nilly. That just 'isn't done' here in the responsible culture of the western world. And all that is just a bunch of hooey (to use the technical term).

The bottom line is that money is associated with virtually every aspect of how you live your life and the decisions you make on a daily basis.

If you need a day off, to take a vacation, to buy a new car, or move to a new home tomorrow, could you do it without thinking about the money? According to widely available statistics, only 1% of us have the ability to do so… and we here in the U.S. live in one of the wealthiest countries in the world!

So what is wrong with this picture? What is it about "handling the paper" that makes our lives go differently than we want? Where do we literally give our life force energy away when it comes to money? The answer is deceptively simple…

Money is just money.

Our true freedom is experienced when we remove all attachments to what money means and realize that making money is just making money. When you release your attachments to money, money has a freedom to be what it is... an energy force. From that place, you can simply choose to just make more money.

Making money mean all the things talked about above is actually a limitation and distorts your relationship with money. Money is just money—and you get to decide how you want to relate to it when you release the unconscious programs currently running you by default.

Money is a powerful creative energy and a generative force that allows possibility to come into being. However, the money itself is really just paper with little symbols on it. Money is a form of creative energy, and when you are in the flow of it, little papers with symbols show up! (Conversely, when you are not in the flow, you do not see a whole lot of it.)

So, paper money and coins are symbols—a reflection—of the energy but not the energy itself. In reality, the money is a delayed symbol of your money energy.

For example, you could have no money but discover you are holding a winning lottery ticket (not yet cashed in). Just knowing you have the ticket is enough to create a new and probably pretty jubilant experience! The same holds true if you have an amazing piece of property, like a yacht or a sports car, but you owe the IRS, who is coming to repossess it tomorrow. Even though you still have that thing, you feel bad. The physical world actually catches up to your money energy.

Knowing that money is a creative energy which yields physical world results in the form of papers and coins with symbols on it, let's explore the eight money lies nobody has talked about openly up until now.

The Eight Money Lies

These money lies are things that have been or are percolating in the back of your mind which make sense but really have not been clearly addressed by traditional conversation, current gurus, or other media.

Some of these might feel like an "oh, yeah, I hadn't thought about that" moment when you take them in…in some cases, they run contrary to popular opinion and, in others, they've not yet been considered but will feel natural as you experience them. It might even be that you feel challenged by some of them; in which case, you will want to take a look at the source of the ping, sting or 'charge' associated with that particular point as an invitation for personal growth.

"What we really want to do is what we are really
meant to do. When we do what we are meant to do,
money comes to us, doors open for us, we feel useful,
and the work we do feels like play to us."
~ Julia Cameron, Author

Money Lie 1:
You Know More Than the Universe

There has been a lot of mainstream attention on the Law of Attraction and using positive affirmations to create what you want in your life. While potentially positive in helping you cultivate a new relationship with your personal manifesting process, some of the tenets of this strategy actually constricts your relationship with Universal, or Source, energy.

For example, when using positive affirmations or intention statements, the general guidance is to be extremely specific about what you want and to always state it in the positive. Accordingly, a sample affirmation statement might look like this:

I am wealthy now, enjoying a million dollars as my income.

At first glance, you might want to refine this affirmation statement to be more solid and even more specific, although it is written in the present tense and 'feels' good. But it doesn't allow "wiggle room" for the Universe to work in 1) terms of the amount (the Universe could bring you more than what you have asked for), 2) the way it's delivered (as income vs. a gift or other source), 3) over what amount of time and 4) there is an underlying supposition that being wealthy is contingent on having that million dollars.

Just because you have not asked with exactly the right words doesn't mean the Universe will be limited in what it brings you.

The Universe knows what you mean and what you are really asking for… remember, this is the system that birthed galaxies! It has created all the moving parts of planets and ecosystems and cellular growth in such a way, from the largest to the smallest measure, that the human mind cannot grasp the complexity. The sun does not forget to rise and the oceans do not forget to wave because we didn't use the right word or didn't say the affirmation in a positive present tense.

The Universe is not listening to your words but to your vibration; that being the case, chances are it knows the difference between a pebble and a mountain, or between a penny and a million dollars.

There IS a very real variable in this conversation, however… that is, all the people on the planet are contributing to the definition of money. So, eight billion people know the difference between a penny and a million dollars but may have different relationships with that concept. Therefore, your co-creative process with the Universe is subjective to the collective definition and, yet, it is not controlled by it. As you gain clarity, your ability to influence your outcomes through a more direct connection supersedes the collective definitions around money.

The Universe also knows what will best serve you. Beyond what you can conceive lies a wide-open vista of possibility you are choosing to either bring forward or experience. The Universe is the creator of all that, as well as the messenger and delivery system that brings 'it' to you. If you simply ask for what you want in alignment with your best and highest good and then get out of the way, chances are your experience will exceed your wildest dreams!

Understand the Universe is listening to all your vibrations. If you say a couple of affirmations for five minutes a day and then spend the rest of the day being angry, grumpy, mad at the world and/or living with a 'lack' mentality, the Universe is picking that up loud and clear. It will bring you experiences to get you to where you want to go but understand they might not feel or look initially to be all that great, because they are resonating at that angry, grumpy, scarce energy level. Attention goes where energy flows. Your vibration speaks louder than your words.

Most likely these experiences are requesting you take action or respond differently than your normal comfort zone. In reality, that makes sense—if the same old stuff you have already been doing was going to get you your dreams, you would have them already. Clearly, a change is required to get you to where you have not been before.

The question is…

> Are you listening to the guidance you are asking to receive from the Universe and which it is giving you to get you to your dreams?

Money Lie 2:
People Always Welcome Having More Money

*"The Sun, with all the planets revolving around it, and
depending on it, can still ripen a bunch of grapes as
though it had nothing else in the Universe to do."*

~ Galileo, Philosopher and Scientist

Even the most positive things in life have an energy that might cause a reaction in you. For example, what if someone handed you five thousand dollars and said it was yours? Your first thought would likely be stunned amazement, then incredulous disbelief and questioning what you have to do for it, then cautious joy, then exuberant delight, and then maybe "oh my gosh, I don't know what to do with it, now I will owe this person, or what if it is stolen?" That is a case of the energetic repulsion, or "charge", to the positive of money in action.

You might not be aware of all the ways you are repelling money energetically when it comes into you and/or you receive it. Pay attention to your first thoughts when you consider receiving a large dollar amount... here are some of the most common ones that are often underestimated as a repellant to receiving and having more money.

- Oh, no thanks—I have enough already.
- What do you mean? I think you have the wrong person.
- What will my friends think? What if they think I'm too good for them now?
- If I get a nicer car, it will be a target for thieves. (And my insurance, maintenance costs, etc. will go up).
- My family is going to want some of my money.
- What if I don't manage it well and waste or lose it?

- I'll have to pay more taxes by being in a higher tax bracket.
- I know how to manage on a budget, but if I'm rich, I'll have more responsibilities.

Do you see yourself in any of these thoughts? If yes, these are unconscious beliefs that are energetically repelling you from receiving and having more money. While they might sound irrational, as in 'who doesn't want more money?', there's a very real energetic component blocking you from having more money. This energy might not be spoken out loud, but the Universe hears it loud and clear. Even more, it will be the energy that comes up if a large sum of money WERE to actually drop into your lap.

Following are some other often hidden beliefs or subversive thoughts that could be causing you to push back on receiving or keeping more money.

- I might want to do things that my friends won't be able to…
- If I move to a nicer house, I'll have to leave my neighborhood and what's familiar.
- People might think I'm snobby if I upgrade my life visibly.
- I'll have to act like a rich person.
- I'm not glamorous enough to have a lot of money.
- I'll have to buy nicer clothes—what if I spill something on them?
- People will see that I'm rich and they'll come after me for it somehow (kidnap my kids, ask for donations, expect gifts, steal from me, etc.).

In each of these cases, you are not allowing yourself to grow into the money and are seeing the challenges of making changes because of having more money, based on unconscious beliefs. Again, these beliefs are formed predominantly as a result of your childhood socialization process through authority figures, like parents, teachers and church members. The good news is, once surfaced, you can choose whether you want to keep these beliefs as an adult.

These unconscious beliefs will no longer have the power to undermine your ability to attract, have and enjoy more money because they are now illuminated for your awareness and decision.

To go further, there are obligations involved in having more money, like managing it well, sharing it appropriately and investing for the future that can be overwhelming. Sometimes people do not know why they received it vs. someone else—for example, it is not fair that someone else didn't win the jackpot or the contest.

Or maybe the source of the money is painful, such as receiving it through a settlement or an inheritance—that carries another level of pain that could result in energetic pushback. It can be seen as being invited or forced to step up and be more powerful in relationship to money. Money is now seen not as something that will get you toys and play time but, rather, as a gift to change your life from someone who cared about you enough to choose you as a beneficiary. With the potential weight of that, you might put out vibration of resistance to having more money—the uber-pushback to more money showing up in your life!

Another concept that undermines having more money is the work ethic that says, 'you have to work hard to earn money'. There are a lot of associations that come along with that statement, like if you did not earn it, you are not good enough and that finding easy money is like cheating the system. For example, there is a cultural pattern that was imprinted into the Western world on a regular basis over the last couple of centuries. It can be summed up as: 'Who are you to not work hard and still expect and enjoy having money?'

The bottom line is it can feel like having more money equals having more responsibility.

That reminds me… I recall seeing a documentary where young aristocrats who inherited large estates with mansions dreaded having old, drafty, creaky large homes with musty antique furniture and old-fashioned artwork that they were expected to maintain. They were also expected to maintain the on-site staff, which meant having to siphon money from their inheritance or generate more income. For them, their wealth was a chain to the past, a drain on their present and a chokehold on their future.

At any rate, if you as a non-aristocrat cannot prove you really worked hard for the money and totally deserve it, you could be judged for having 'easy' money. Your lifestyle changes and there is actually less freedom associated with having more money—again, these are limitations and another potential source of the energetic repulsion to more money.

Money Lie 3:
Your Personal Evolution Is Related to Your Money

"Money is only a tool. It will take you wherever you wish,
but it will not replace you as the driver."

~ Ayn Rand, Author

Many popular gurus and self-help guides teach that as you evolve, so will your money. But that does not explain the people who might have money who are not good people (you know who we mean here), nor does it explain why good people do not have money.

In fact, your money is not static—it is a dynamic, changing reflection of your money energy. However, it is important to know it is ONLY a reflection of your money energy... where you are spiritually is independent of your money energy (although it is influenced by it).

Think of it this way... money is a thermostat within your house, but it is not your house nor is it really relevant to the value of your house. You might have a million-dollar home that is cold because your thermostat is not working or cannot keep up with your heating needs, or you might have a little old shanty that's warm. Your house is your evolution and the thermostat / heat in your house is your money attraction—and, just as in your home, while they are in the same general area, they are independent of each other and have different functions but are still related. If your house has tons of holes or leaks in it, then a lot more heat (money energy) is going to be needed to keep it warm.

Now, your money attraction could be easier as you evolve and develop personally, but it is not contingent upon your personal development. In fact, one of the houses might support heat better—maybe your shanty is leaky and poorly constructed—but you have the ability to adjust your thermostat accordingly. Likewise, if you have a home that is beautiful on the outside but is not well-constructed, that is also a problem as your thermostat cannot keep up. But you are in charge of your thermostat, so it can change depending on how you define the circumstances.

In reality, it is nice to be warm wherever you are, right? You can be on the beach or in a public place and activate your thermostat with a bonfire or additional clothing layers. The same is true for your money attraction thermostat—you can adjust it independent of your evolution (i.e., your house).

Moncy Lie 4:
People Are Willing to Receive Wealth

"When you change the way you look at things, the things you look at change."
~ Max Planck, Nobel Prize-winning physicist

To receive money takes action on any individual's part to accommodate it showing up. Without a willingness to be open to receiving, or to allowing it to enter without attachment to the source, you are literally constricting your money flow. If you do not create the space for money to show up in your life with open arms and willingness to receive, just like welcoming a friend into your home, it is not going to show up. The Universe is listening to the vibrations you are not verbalizing.

So how do you know when you don't have a 'willingness' for wealth? The sure-fire tell-tale sign is you are not taking actions to remove the blocks to attracting and receiving money. This can be both transcendental (that is, on the energetic plane) but also physically (on the mundane plane, right here right now).

For example, if you find yourself wanting more money, but not investing in your skills to attract or manage it, you are demonstrating a lack of willingness to partner with and welcome wealth. If you look around to see your environment is shabby, filled with items that look or feel like poverty, or filled with clutter, you are not creating space for money flow in your life. Rather, you are reminding yourself to stay stuck in not having as much money as you want.

Here is another example... are you willing to do door-to-door sales? As in, knocking on people's doors to introduce a product in exchange for their business? It is less about the actual act, but if you are willing to do something like that, you have a willingness to wealth. And most people do not have it—they have a resistance to doing something that doesn't align with what they deem appropriate. Where are you resisting money in a way that you would enjoy the process but there is an unconscious resistance telling you no no NO?

Your blocks to taking willing action are actually blocks preventing your access to and attraction of money. The act of resistance to be willingly open to money is unconscious self-sabotage that is insidious, hidden and creates behavioral challenges on the physical level. Now that's a big statement but that is determining your end result with regard to money.

So take a moment to think about where you are not demonstrating a willingness to welcome wealth... and consider that your action plan to make some changes right away!

Money Lie 5:
Giving Is About Helping Other People

> *"You have not lived a perfect day, even though you have earned your money, unless you have done something for someone who will never be able to repay you."*
>
> ~ Ruth Smeltzer, Contemporary Philosopher

One of the more interesting aspects of money is giving it to worthy causes or people as a donation or tithing (the difference being that tithing is a set and consistent amount given to a source of spiritual growth or inspiration). There is a shadow side to giving, which is what we are going to explore here.

The determining factor of the shadow side of giving is really your degree of consciousness and intention for giving in the first place. If you are giving out of a sense of obligation, or worse, false obligation, you want to notice what you are getting from your gift. Does your giving provide you will the vibration of feeling abundance, happy, feel, or excited? Or does it make you feel vulnerable, being controlled, cheated, in scarcity?

Giving can be a great way, as an access point, to get you into those feelings as a vibration that helps you feel good which creates more circumstances to feeling good. However, giving does not intrinsically cause this—if giving makes you feel 'negative' in some way, you are only going to get more 'negative' in return.

There are times when giving actually reinforces the other person's lack consciousness or buys into their deficiencies in being able to generate money for themselves. You give them money because they cannot do it on their own… you can see this with parents who are overly generous with adult children. That is not to say parents should not give to their children; rather, it is an example where their over-generosity is impairing or even sabotaging their adult children's growth opportunities.

And then there is the trap of giving as a means to feel superior to someone who is weaker or who has less than you at the moment. In that case, the underlying reason you give is because you are feeling inferior. With this dynamic present, the reality is you are feeling the need to feel superior to someone. The recipient of your gift is simply a mirror to your feelings of inferiority. And remember, the universe is listening to that vibration.

Some people say you need to give to get. In fact, that is a distortion of truth because making money is not about giving. Making money is not a transaction and there is no expectation that needs to be attached to giving.

Generating money is really about your ability to receive.

When you give a gift purely for the joy of giving, you get the chance to experience (or receive) the feeling of that joy and then attract more joy. There is not a standard of giving that needs to be met for you to be able to start receiving.

Donations and giving can be a great vehicle to train you to receive the great feelings that come from giving, but you still have to be willing to engage your spirit, connect to the feelings associated with giving and allow it to happen. Giving is a great way to demonstrate your ability to receive; if you are not able to receive, the natural cycle is broken and money generation is likewise obstructed. You are actually giving for your own benefit, so make sure to look at what you are receiving as a result of your giving.

Be sure to consider the associations you have in your mind or heart when giving—if you give but fear you won't have enough money for yourself, that energy will permeate and perpetuate that as a reality in the physical world. If you are giving but feel like you are losing, then that is what will be sustained in your life. Conversely, if it feels good to give, it makes your life even more positive and abundant.

It is what you're getting from your giving that supports your money energy.

Essentially, there is not a giant cosmic bank account that you're depositing into and building for yourself (karmically or otherwise). The point of giving is to shift your vibration from scarcity while helping others through your sharing of your ability to generate money. However, you do not need to give to vibrate at abundance. Giving is a tool but it does not have an inherent value. The real value of giving is in assessing your energetic state throughout the process of giving.

Money Lie 6:
People Know How to Value Money

"Don't tell me where your priorities are. Show me where you spend your money and I'll tell you what they are."

~ James W. Frick, Philanthropist

This is one of the more interesting, and difficult to explain, money lies—that people know how to value money. It is (amazingly enough) not true for a lot of people. Money is valued when it is inappropriate AND money is over-simplified when it should not be—both of which hold a lot of energy around people's experiences with money.

Physical world symptoms of the dichotomy of money show up when people think money is part (or cause or reward) of their personal evolution, that they can make more money with less ethics, or that money doesn't matter with spending splurges on credit. Money has been disrespected as an individual creative force in each of these situations.

Think of money as water… water has no shape unless it has a vessel to hold it. Whether growing yourself solely for the result of making money, when sacrificing your personal values or ignoring the consequences of taking on debt, you are crafting your water / money vessel to lack structural integrity through each of those actions. It will not be able to do a good job of holding your money or of supporting you generating more money to put in it.

You can create bigger wealth, but just making money does not mean your vessel is growing. Your money can outgrow your vessel. This explains why people make or win lots of money and then lose it—they did not pay attention to the vessel. And just because you grow your vessel does not mean your money is growing. Your wealth is independent of your vessel, and yet relies on it to harness the power of attracting more and having it.

As stated previously, money is a neutral force, and a generative force in its own right, but it becomes mutated when weight is assigned to it in the wrong places.

A financial splurge is not necessarily bad, but it takes on a different value if you actually needed to buy food or other life necessities. This is not about judgment—it is about honoring the relationship you have to money and your priorities.

Money is important but not in the way most people consider it to be, as exemplified by doing the 'right' things or growing yourself spiritually and using money as the measure of your progress. It is actually saying money is more than what it is in that example. There is a confusion that happens with money not being valued properly. People get hooked by thinking they are making money and so they must be doing right things. It is a false standard to associate with, and measure, life progress.

When people are in a money-deficient state, and then shrug off money as being not important somehow ("oh, whatever… I don't need it… I'm fine… I didn't want to do that anyway, money doesn't matter", etc.), that is a placebo to help them feel better about the gap between the money they need and the money that is immediately available to them. It is a way for them to mentally cope, but it is a dysfunctional way to avoid looking at reality. By living in 'lack' and discrediting money, they continue to not attract, create, have, or enjoy more money.

Following is an analogy for considering money as a fuel source.

Think of stacking bricks. Plain, regular, run-of-the-mill bricks. You can use those bricks to build a beautiful church or mansion OR you can just stack bricks in any old way. You could get caught in how many bricks are stacked or how they are stacked—in either case, that is a waste of time but you are still caught in that because you are missing the bigger picture. You are caught up in the measurables you have in that moment to evaluate your progress. It is the same with money… "look at how much I made today" is an example. The money is not the bricks (or in your day's take); rather, money is the energy that moved the bricks to become a beautiful building (or contribute to a larger outcome through your day's productivity).

The bricks were the fuel source for a final product, but they do not have generative, creational, inherent value in and of themselves until they became a tangible expression of the energy that moved them. Having piles of bricks has no real value on its own, but there is a value to it once there is a tangible result that could happen only by using them. It is the energy of using the bricks that moves the building evolution forward, just as the energy of money moves you forward to your life goals. Discounting the bricks as not valuable because they do not have their own value would be a mistake, just as discounting money as only little pieces of paper with symbols would be a mistake.

Another facet of this dichotomy of money is to consider money as oxygen. Oxygen is widely available, but you cannot really sell it. However, if you do not have oxygen, you are going to have a big problem.

Money is also everywhere—like oxygen—and has the potential

for you to use it to create change. However, people think they do not have access to it, or somehow cannot tap into it consistently.

Sometimes they start collecting money to feel secure in having something. But collecting for the sake of collecting it is not valuable, and, in fact, reinforces a lack mentality. There is a desire to store up potential in case it might be needed or wanted later, but that signifies a disbelief in the idea of infinite supply. And if nothing is ever done with the stored potential, there exists a hoarding issue—a clear indicator the cycle of abundance is not working. It is not about generating something but more about not losing something that does not really have value in the way that is commonly believed.

What would it be like if there were an ocean that was dammed up, with floodgates that could open to fill up smaller lakes connected to it? If you were the owner of those smaller lakes, you would likely be happy about that. Over time, you might even come to believe the floodgates are your key to having your lake filled up. In truth, if and when that should occur, you have lost your connection to the possibility of owning the ocean—your focus has narrowed to the floodgates and the little lake that needs to be filled up, when the little lake doesn't really matter. You could be accessing the ocean anytime you want but you get caught up with filling up your lake and then getting more lakes to fill and then more lakes to fill because you want the water, must have the water in case you might need it for something.

You constantly experience the lack of water and you never get the joy of doing something with the water. The biggest loss is you not realizing you can have all the water you ever want or need by letting go of the lakes and claiming the ocean.

The big question….

What if you had an ocean and unlimited supply of water—what would you now want to do with it?

And the possibly even bigger question…

Would you be willing to leave your familiar little lake behind in order to claim the ocean?

Money Lie 7: People Know What to Pay Attention to With Money

"What difference does it make how much you have?
What you do not have amounts to much more."

~ Seneca, Philosopher and Statesman

Most people tend to focus on their corner of the world—what they can do to create money, working with what they know as a form to generate money. Sometimes that is a job, sometimes that is a particular business service, sometimes it is relying on family fortune. The unfortunate part of that is that it actually keeps people stuck and limited to what they already know and what they've already experienced. They are missing the real show.

The real show is the infinite supply of money that is always available to you (and everyone else) and connecting to that cleanly and clearly while being open to the new possibilities and forms that emerge through that connection to help you grow yourself in relation to that infinite source. That is a mouthful so let's expand on that for a minute.

Think of a child who gets a double-scoop ice cream cone, leaves the store in triumph, licks it too hard and the ice cream goes 'thump' on the sidewalk because the child did not know how to manage all that ice cream. We do the same thing with money—we ask for a lot of money, but then do not demonstrate that we know how to handle it. The error comes when we judge ourselves as wrong for what happened, instead of simply going back and getting another double or even triple scoop and trying it again. We get judged or judge ourselves as we "can't handle it" and make ourselves smaller, take on less, diminish our power. If you think about it, to handle a double-decker, what better way than to try handling the triple-scoop, right? But so often we hold ourselves back, don't push ourselves and don't give ourselves enough credit for being able to handle something bigger (especially if we experience what we would deem a failure somehow).

We need to grow ourselves in proportion to the amount of money we want to physically manifest. If we stick with what we know, we don't grow. And if we focus only on the ice cream (i.e., the money), we're missing the point.

The idea is to consider our connection points, or our access to the infinite supply of money, vs. only focusing on the money.

Energy is dynamic and constantly in a state of change. And so are our connection points to money. But we will miss discovering those emerging connection points if we continue to do what we've always done, or limit our growth, which is the 'real show'.

It is possible for you to increase your capacity to attract and handle more money not because you don't already have that, but rather, because your limitations are in the way and they are constricting how much money energy you can receive. By releasing your limitations, you are growing your ability to see and connect with your access points to infinite money.

It's exciting to grow and match the vibration of what is always available to us in terms of money.

You could focus on the latest fad, technique, or strategy, but you're actually missing your own show. You could be tapped into infinite abundance right now if you pay attention to your own dynamic connection points. Consider these as personal invitations to grow! We are not meant to stay stuck at any particular level (in really any part of our lives)—we are living, breathing, dynamic organisms! And that includes going up or going down—the limitation is our judgment that down is bad with an admonition of "don't do that", which causes the fear of "losing" and, as a result, the rigor mortis sets in.

We are designed to grow, expand and be more, be less… and the reward for and in that kind of positive momentum is access to everything we need to make our growth happen.

So, if you are focused only on your ice cream, or you're looking at what you've always done, or looking back at what you've accomplished, or using someone else's connection points, or trying to connect to an access point that is no longer available, or you're unaware of the possibilities that are presenting to you on a continual basis, you're going to energetically block your money. You're missing the huge potential that could open for you... you're missing the real show—your own access to your own infinite money supply.

Money Lie 8:
You Need to Build a Cash Machine

"Money is neither my god nor my devil. It is a form of energy that tends to make us more of who we already are, whether it's greedy or loving."

~ Dan Millman, Author

This last money lie might prove to be one of the most pivotal and complex of all. Here it is... there is no need for you to go out and build a new cash machine for yourself because it is already waiting for you.

Let's explore this... assuming you are here as a physical expression of divine consciousness, you are a part of a much greater whole. In fact, that whole contains all potential as well as current physical manifestation. To take that one step further, because you are a part of the greater whole, which contains the all of creation, you are already the money which you desire to have and your connection to that money is already established. It is only your ability to clear what is in the way of your money that is the issue.

Said another way, once you clear your limitations to wealth, including conditioned patterns of thinking, self-sabotaging behaviors, negative self-talk, projects, judgment and unconscious decision based on hidden beliefs, your access to what is already you and yours is revealed and, simultaneously, is received by you. Just like a boulder in a river clogs up the flow of the river, your limitations are constricting your access to your personal cash machine.

An example of a limitation in action might be if you decide to upgrade your vehicle, but somewhere feel like you won't be able to afford it, others might judge you for making that decision, or you want a sports car instead of a hybrid vehicle. Those underlying beliefs will permeate the process of buying the new car, and, ultimately, your ability to have and enjoy it.

The good news is you do not need to build a cash machine! However, the flip side is most people have an attachment to money as a thing or an end to getting what they want. They either need money—which is a scarcity mentality and experience—or they are disconnected from the concept that they are already connected to an infinite money supply, or they do not know they already possess their cash machine. In the latter case, what that means is that they feel pressure to take some external action, however, the most powerful action is an internal shift.

Know your cash machine is already available to you and that, by clearing your limitations, conditioned thinking, and self-sabotaging patterns, you can access all the money you want easily and effortlessly.

And There You Have It…
A Summary

A quick summary of the eight money lies in the following statements.

Money Lie 1: You Know More Than the Universe

This lie is demonstrated by the statement: "The Universe doesn't know the difference between and penny and a million dollars…" The universe listens to your vibration(s)—all of them—and is always bringing you your energetic match, even potentially exceeding your expectations in bring you what is in your best and highest good. The universe is on your side; the hard part is that you, like many of us, sometimes do not realize that you, yourself, are not.

Money Lie 2: People Always Welcome Having More Money

People are unconsciously pushing away money with thought -rules, such as: more money equals more responsibility, more judgment, etc.

Money Lie 3: Your Personal Evolution Is Related to Your Money

Your spiritual growth is independent of your relationship with money.

Money Lie 4: People Are Willing to Receive Wealth

Receiving money takes both action and willingness on your part to accommodate it showing up.

Money Lie 5: Giving Is About Helping Other People

Your intention and positive feelings as a result of donating or tithing is a determining factor in your ability to generate more money.

Money Lie 6: People Know How to Value Money

Put the appropriate emphasis and respect for money in the right places—money is the generative energy that can make valuable things happen.

Money Lie 7: People Know What to Pay Attention to With Money

Going beyond what you know and have already done to cultivate and enhance your connection places to money energetically.

Money Lie 8: You Need to Build A Cash Machine

As a physical representation of all that is in creation, you already are your cash machine—remove your limitations to it and you can access it vs. thinking you need to build one.

Your Greatness Waits for You

The key is to energetically open yourself to your own vital connection points which, in some cases, have never been accessed before but are destined only for you. Your greatness always waits for you.

By taking in and contemplating each of these money lies and how to address them differently, you are already illuminating your challenge points around attracting, creating, and enjoying 'the having' of more money.

The Triggers, Limitations, Co-Dependency and Responsibilities of Money

Exploring Your Energy Around Money

This book is intended to explore the energy around money, much of it as programming throughout the ages related to various perception of it. These perceptions include not having enough of it, as well as the triggers, limitations, co-dependency with and responsibilities of money which could be greatly affecting your ability to receive money and how you feel when the money actually does show up.

As you begin to open up and understand the nuances of how money stimulates you and your response to it, you give yourself renewed power to create a new relationship with wealth.

Many of the concepts presented in this book will likely reference parts of your relationship with money to which you are unconscious. And by being unconscious to it, you are in reaction to money versus being in a powerful, dynamic "oneness" with it. "Oneness" is a term that connotes a closeness that goes beyond a "relationship", which, by definition, describes the distance between two things. By being in oneness with money, there is no separation between you and your money—you are abundance and wealth is you.

In working with the information presented here, take time to integrate the teachings in how they relate to you. The key is not necessarily the information itself, but your response to what you read and the perceptions that come to the surface of your awareness. Ideally, you will discover your "hooks", or those points of your being that are out of alignment and, therefore, offer a resting place for non-supporting thoughts, behaviors and actions related to money.

Your Money Hooks are Resistance

Often, it is our "hooks" that embody resistance to new ideas and will kick off what we perceive as negative emotions like anger, resentment, or unexplained emotional "flummox", and / or a sense of being out of sorts (among other responses). As you consider your triggers, limitations, and relationship with money, you are releasing stuck energy. Just as there cannot be dark where there is light, stuck energy cannot exist where there is movement. Your proactive consideration of your stuck energy places is enough to help it begin to dissipate.

Your limitations are the most fertile place from which to create intentional change. It is not until you know your limitations that you can know where to begin doing something different. Just like you need to know where you are to get to a new destination on a road trip, you need to understand your limitations. Essentially, limitations are the progressive steppingstones to your goals, as you understand and unlock the growth opportunity contained in them.

There is Magic in Your Limitation

There is a magic in your limitations not found anywhere else in the whole of the Universe, because they are comprised of your particular "Earth School" lessons, with the variables only you bring to the curriculum. Thank the teachers who show up for you because you have called them in for instruction. These teachers may seem to be unlikely guides… usually they are the people (and situations) who challenge you the most, because that is where your greatest potential lies.

Your soul knows this and, as you send out the signal for those teachings to come in to you (think radio station emitting a signal), you will challenge yourself to go beyond what you are used to on a regular basis. You (like every other human) tend to continue to do what is familiar, regardless of whether it's working for you or not, and the signal from the Universe is there to break you out of the 'curse' of the familiar.

Through your increased perceptions, you will be intentionally shifting your relationship with money.

You will likely notice having different experiences as a result of your newfound clarity so even routine activities, like balancing your checkbook, will yield new insights to you. Remember to not judge yourself for previous habits or knowledge (or lack of it); had you known better then, you would have done better.

Also, as you shift your relationship with money, you are shifting your relationship with the world around you and the people in it. While they will likely experience new growth as well, they will notice your shifts and mirror them back to you. The Universe is always giving you messages; reflections from others is just one way you will gain information about your personal growth journey.

As you read this information, notice where you get "lit up", or emotionally engaged, and follow that as your next opportunity in creating a new relationship with wealth.

Consider Your Triggers and Limitations

Let's start with exploring triggers and limitations. As previously mentioned, a trigger is something that stings, pings or has a 'charge', and may eventually lead to some other behavior or thought pattern than desired. A single word can "trigger" a reaction of some sort; it feels a bit like an instinctual knee jerk reaction. For example, when someone is having a bad day, it can trigger road rage, a spending splurge, or an argument with a complete stranger in an attempt to discharge the energy and to try to feel better in that moment.

A limitation is a stuck choice, and generally shows itself as a misidentification or misapplication when you feel like there isn't a choice in a given situation. For example, when a person feels they have to stay in a job because they are making good money, they are experiencing a self-imposed limitation. This is really a case of misidentification of the fear they may have in leaving the job, despite being as unhappy as they are, for an unknown and uncertain future.

Generally speaking, triggers and limitations around money tend to run to the negative at first glance. Here is a common one—if you don't have enough money, you aren't successful. However, there is no magic number that signifies that you are now actually successful. It's a dynamic standard of measurement, so the number is always moving, depending on your life situation. And even if you attain "it", whatever that number is, it won't make you feel successful.

Success is a state of mind, not a number in your bank account.

Feeling Successful Is a Choice

At the moment, you (and most humans) likely have energetic blocks in the way, which affect what you create in the world. However, in the end, it will come down to choosing to feel successful simply because you choose it. This choice will greatly contribute to your ease in creating what you want. Ultimately, you are choosing to have the experience you are having and, whether your choice is success or not success, there isn't a right or wrong to it. It's your choice and how you feel about it that matters.

Following are some of the more common triggers and limitations that keep people stuck.

> If your debt is too high, you're not successful… you need to pay your debt off before doing anything else… you have to be "responsible" about having a job… however, it's all about how you perceive your debt and the meaning you attach to it. If you buy into any of these above interpretations, then you are creating a defended point of view that keeps you attached to wanting to be right and creating situations that prove you are right in what you think you know. If you are committed to believing that debt is a horrible thing, and you have debt, it's fairly certain you will start having debt show up as horrible. The key to freedom is locating where you misidentified and misapplied what debt means to you.

Another trigger is that what's in your checking account is a measure of the money you have and/or a measure of your success… in fact, what's in your checking account is just what is in your checking account. It changes frequently, depending on what you are depositing and paying out, or even when you are recording your transactions. For example, when you deposit money into an ATM machine, many banks will take up to three days to actually put the money into your account, but your checkbook register shows the money to be there. Your checking account is not a stable measure of the money you have, and it certainly can't measure your success, financial or otherwise.

There are people with a huge bank balance but who still don't feel successful. There are also people with negative bank balances and they feel unsuccessful. What's a little uncanny is that the reverse is also true—it's possible that someone can have no money in the bank but still feel successful or, in contrast, have a lot of money in the bank and feel unsuccessful. Clearly, a self-imposed and energetic limitation is in place and running amuck. In either case, the actual amount of money is irrelevant—it is the personal choice of the account holder that determines their experience.

Wealth Generation Potential

The bank account balance also doesn't take into consideration your wealth generation potential—it can only reflect a small snapshot of what's happening with your finances at any given moment. It is merely a "print-out" of your money energy, showing the end result of your energy. It is not the cause of your money energy. AND there is also a delay in you actually receiving the money, depending on how the physical world processes your money energy.

The good news is that, if your bank account is low, you can change the energy to change your bank account balance.

How much money your friends have, or how much money you perceive they have, is an impossible situation for you to know… because it's not possible for you to know the truth of their situation— nor does it matter. You could easily choose new friends who are doing much better or much worse by your perception, and your data to measure success would change accordingly. Just because something looks a particular way doesn't make it so… people choose to relate with and spend their money in very personal ways. Those who determine having a nice wardrobe may spend credit to get it but look successful.

In the western world, the socialization process is to not talk about money, so chances are people don't tell the whole truth about their money. People will show you only what they are comfortable with seeing for themselves, which is a clue as to what's really happening for them if you can perceive it (as well as for you, because it's your mirror).

Whatever is happening "out there" is merely a reflection of what's happening for you on the "inside".

How much your family has OR thinks you have... parents and families tend to believe their children adopt the same money values and make financial decisions the same way they did when growing up—it's just human nature. However, it isn't necessarily true. In fact, people may actually rebel, pushing back those values in resistance by doing the opposite. Whether you are in blind acceptance or in active resistance through rebellion and doing the opposite, you are a victim to this trigger. It is causing you to do something you aren't doing in conscious clarity for your best and highest good.

One of my clients would not post pictures celebrating her financial achievements—a new car or home—because her mother would question them. Another client downplayed her wealth, including having a second home and her own plane, because she did not want to brag about money to her family who had less money.

Passing up a parent's financial earning capacity could be a limitation you have but it is also not related to your parents' actual earning capacity. You may not have accurate figures to work with about their income because it is 'dated' for their generation with different economies and inflation. Additionally, parents have wildly different financial thresholds from household to household. If you thought you mom/dad made only $40K, but they actually made $100K and you adopted to not make more than them, you would end up choosing $40K as your limit even though it wasn't their limit—you just thought it was their limit. Once again, you created your own limitation based on perception, so it's not true. It is also not right or wrong—it is only a choice that most people don't want to acknowledge they have made.

There's a lot of judgment in this one—if you go beyond the apparent earning capacity of one or both of your parents, that could mean they weren't enough or you might make them look bad or you'll need to take care of them. So not only does the self-judgment not support you but it takes an emotional toll. It's a different time with different economies so your results are likely to be very different from theirs. Your parents had (have) their own relationship to money, and, in fact, may have more money than they shared with you, so you might not have a clear picture of the total earning capacity anyway. In this case, you're constricting your money capacity back based on fiction.

Your Pathway to Freedom

In any case, your new freedom comes from not buying any of the limitations as real and clearing out the energy blocks. In the end, it is the energy blocks that stop you and, once you are stopped, it's probable you look and misidentify that something in the physical world was the cause when it was actually the energy that blocked your results.

Another misidentification people make is to give into parental pressures on making financial choices. However, no one can make choices for you—they can influence you but only you make your choices. Even as a child, if you think you did not know you had a choice, that's a misidentification of information.

In order to facilitate going forward, 'own' everything that has happened in your life.

Own It to Grow Through It

When you claim that you made the choices which got you to where you find yourself today, you empower yourself to create what you want going forward. The limitations of the past turn simply turn into choices that are easily and instantly changed.

Another key is to not judge those choices as being right or wrong, unless you want to "fix" them (as in, make them permanent) and limit what you can choose in the future. Again, it would not be a right or wrong thing; this is simply another choice to lock yourself into living from the past. Sometimes that can mean 'owning' some apparently unattractive life options, like abusive childhoods or traumatic events. However, those very circumstances helped to make you who you are as you navigated your way through them. See the magic in where you made the choices so you could survive—and 'own' that you did!

In this particular case of life ownership, you chose your mother and/or father before you came into the world, which is your original power choice in the relationship. For any given situation, you could have said no to the option presented to you, you could have taken action to give yourself more opportunities, you could have negotiated other options… in any case, there is a reason your parents are your parents. And your current financial situation and choices, past and present, are not about your parents.

Limitations are ways you define yourself based on the money you have and manifest as making money something that it isn't … for example, if you misidentify or misapply that having money means you aren't connected to your Source, or that not having money means you are doing God's work, either thought pattern will greatly affect your ability to receive money and enjoy the process.

A limitation is a stuck choice, which makes you think it's fixed and un-changing. Once the energy around it gets unstuck, it is back to being simply a choice and now you (and the situation) have the freedom to be without attachment to some default mode of being. You can simply make a new choice.

Avoid the Control of Money

One of the biggest triggers and / or limitations around money is when it is used as a control mechanism.

Money is a powerful generative force, and when someone has access to a lot of money by being aligned with their money energy, they are perceived as powerful. Conversely, those who do not have the same access to money may perceive themselves as not being powerful (and, therefore, others do as well). They 'bought' their lack of power as real, and, as a result, they create money as a manipulative tool in relationships.

Money is just an energy and what is done with that energy is up to the ALL the people involved—the group effects the creation of the outcome.

Where have you gone unconscious around money?

What limitations appear as permanent to you?

Your (Potential) Co-Dependency with Money

Co-dependency is generally defined as a coping strategy that includes compulsive behaviors in relationship as a response to either another person or a stressor. Over time, co-dependency affects self-image and social independence as the person engages in an abuse cycle (for example, over-giving and experiencing an inability to improve the situation).

There are various symptoms that show up as a co-dependence… controlling behaviors, perfectionism, distrust, avoidance of feelings, hyper-vigilance, excessive attention, physical illness, depression, or extreme frustration. In the case of money, money either becomes an enabler of the person who is creating the situation by using money as something other than what it is, OR, money becomes the victim of an abuse cycle as the person makes compromises and limits their possibilities due to their distorted perceptions around the money they have or don't have or choose to spend in a particular way.

An example of co-dependence in a money scenario is someone who uses making a lot of money to reinforce that s/he isn't "enough" somehow, which engages a cycle of self-abuse. His/her self-confidence is predicated on how much money s/he has in the bank, so s/he is attached to his/her bank account as the expression of his/her worth. However, there is a twist. The more money s/he makes, the worse s/he feels, so s/he then starts to pound on down the make more money path in desperation to make more and more money while losing everything else in his/her life. The result of making money actually serves to make him/her feel like s/he is "less" and compels him/her to make more money all because money was misidentified as something it is not.

Conversely, someone else may use not making money as a reason to keep themselves small and lack the feeling of success. They will desperately drive after money and then sabotage themselves before they get it as a means to reinforce their misidentification about money.

As you can see, whether you make a lot of money or not, money is just money—the only meaning it has is what you give it.

The Limitation Isn't the Money

Another example of money co-dependence is the feeling you are limited because you do not have enough money. In this case, it is actually your energy which dictates the number of opportunities available to you. For someone who is "locked" into a job because of the "golden handcuffs" of making a nice salary, this person is using money to hide the fear of leaving the job, as well as (in all likelihood) uncovering and claiming their greatness. Money is used as the cause to block receiving new opportunities and avoid seeing the greatness of their essential being.

It is easy to blame money for what's happening when, in reality, we are using money to mask what we don't want to look at in our lives.

Likewise, a stereotypical example of this would be the woman who stays married, albeit unhappily, ostensibly for the money. She's using money for security but she wants her husband for a host of other reasons, with money being the "cover" for her aversion to change—the attachment she has to her lifestyle, the power exchange that occurs as a result of their money dynamic ("bribes", spending decisions, or others as examples) and more. She could look at this as being "trapped" in the relationship, but he could also feel "trapped" in the marriage as well... again, when something can be true from both sides of the proverbial coin, there is a limitation at work.

Essentially, if you have reached a place in your life where money is the controlling factor in your decision-making, when it is the ruler of your life, and if you are compromising who you are for money, it's time to start re-shaping your relationship with your wealth. Who would you be without worrying about money?

'Reverse-engineer' your money energy—begin with feeling where you want to be as though it were today and then act to match your energy with that vibration.

The Responsibilities of Having Money

There is a mystique to having more money; part of that mystique occurs when you attain a certain level of wealth—you are supposed to make certain decisions or behave in a particular "new" way.

For example, if a person has a lot of money, they are supposed to magically manage it better, invest it well, protect it, take care of family and others, and/or live a different lifestyle. But the same holds true if you don't have money… you need to manage it better, invest it well, protect it, take care of family and others, and/or live a particular lifestyle. Even within one side or the other, there exists misidentifications; for example, if you have a lot of money, you don't need to manage it because you have so much!

When something can happen or look the same from either side, there is a limitation at work.

Many people make money a "cause" of how they are living their life versus the money being an "effect". Think of it like this… you type gibberish in your computer and print it out, but what is printed is gibberish so you blame the computer for being dysfunctional. In reality, the print-out is a reflection of how you used the computer—there isn't anything wrong with the computer, the printer or the print-out. In this case, your money is a print-out, just like everything else in your world, of what you're creating through your energy, choices, and actions.

If you wait to have enough money to be able to enjoy life vs. enjoying life and being open to your money energy, you will have vastly different life experiences. And neither is good or bad… it's whether you want it the way you are experiencing it or not. You are at choice in how you relate to your money; there is no inherent law you are breaking when you make one choice or another (unless it involves choosing to rob a bank …). ;+)

At any rate, no one else can dictate your responsibilities with money—only you choose your lifestyle, how you spend money, how you feel about the money that comes into your life. If you are "supposed" to be living a different lifestyle, you have the unique ability among sentient beings to proactively create it. We as a collective culture are in a time of ultimate freedom in many ways, and even more so when we recognize our ability to manifest intentionally.

Knowing what you know, you no longer get to say that things "happen" to you.

You Alone Create Your Experience

No one else is responsible for how you are living your life and accepting your responsibilities. You are creating your experience.

Here is another example of cause and effect that isn't as immutable as one would think—gravity. If you fall on earth, you fall down and would, ultimately, end up at the center of the earth due to gravity. However, if you were deep in space far away from large objects, like planets, moon, and suns, and fell "down", it would not happen— there would not be a strong pull of gravity on you. So, there is not a truth to falling down… and the same is true with money.

When you have money, you can use it to make you feel responsible or you can use not making money to feel responsible. The amount and level of responsibility is what you deem appropriate for you with the lifestyle you are choosing to lead.

The most responsible thing you can do is cultivate your wealth energy vibration. By attuning your wealth frequency with abundance, there will be a significant impact on your life (and on that of the people around you). Reading this book is one way to help clear energetic "gunk" around your relationship with money.

Another is to understand where your money "hooks" are so you know where you are, or where you go unconscious, in your relationship with money.

Third is to uncover where you have mis-identified money or made it into something other than it is; by illuminating these areas, you allow yourself to gain a new freedom about money.

It is also important to feeeeeel the vibration of wealth you are currently experiencing and, as you begin to recognize what it feels like to be abundant, it will be easier to maintain that vibration and have the experience of being wealthy. Doing so will allow you to get rid of or shift what does not feel wealthy in your life, because that is an anchor to the very experience you desire to have… think of it as an energetic detox!

Be responsible—enjoy the wealth!

Myths and Fears You Might Have About Money

Money holds a lot of power and energy for people and, therefore, it generates many fears for people. One of the biggest curses (along with sex) is money. There is a desire to go after it and, once you actually get it, you may be deemed as bad or wrong for having it. Over time, those fears consolidate into a shared experience that becomes part of culture as myths or urban legends. (Wealthy people are selfish, wealthy people are jerks, wealthy people are snobs, etc.—and who wants to be any of those things?)

One of the most active myths occurring at the moment is that the global economy dictates one's personal financial condition. What most people do not realize is you would have to see yourself as separate from the global economy to be at its effect. Since we are all part of the economy and the economy is just the sum total of what we are all creating, the global economy exists at the effect of us. When you decide to receive more wealth, you are, effectively, the catalyst that increases the wealth in the global economy. When you decide to receive less, you are also the catalyst to decreasing the global economy. You are always in control and the global economy is just the physical representation, or print-out, of the level at which everyone's collective energy is resonating.

The global economy is a giant overview of people's issues, functioning as a giant collective mirror of the beliefs of all the people. Think of it as a big thermometer that measures the pulse of people's financial attitudes and energy. If it is negative enough, then it becomes perpetuated by communication systems that benefit by sharing such information, such as news media. Media stories reinforce people's negative paradigms, which—since the beginning of the trade economy—are known as a major power source to marketers and which serves to generate revenues for and from advertisers.

People personalize the global economy to be their experience, but they do not realize they are making the choice to do so.

Money Is Not Separate—But It Is Meaningless

Another commonly accepted myth is that money is separate from people but, without people, money would be meaningless. Remember that people generate money energy, which is what creates the value of money. Without money energy, money would be paper with symbols on it, just like any other computer print-out or newspaper or brochure. We humans are the ones assigning the value to money, so it is impossible for money to exist as something valuable apart from us.

There is a pervasive myth that the rich get richer and the poor get poorer, but that doesn't explain the celebrities or lottery winners who lose their money overnight or the disadvantaged underdog who "makes good". While this may be true, it's not true for the reason most people ascribe to it. For example, there is a misidentification here (among many) that it takes money to make money, which isn't true because a stack of money set in a particular place by itself doesn't multiply or duplicate itself on its own.

It also presupposes there is a limitation on the people who seem to have more obstacles to overcome; yet, all that is really evident is their alignment with their money energy. It doesn't presume they are good people (as evidenced by drug dealers becoming wealthy by taking advantage of people's addictions).

Conversely, rich people don't need to be "good" people to be worthy of being wealthy and, yet, they often appear to be getting richer. Both these opinions are based on personal judgments rather than fact and have, over time, become fixed in people's minds as paradigms passed down through generations—the result of which becomes a myth is born.

Generally speaking, money fears tap into the very core of survival issues.

Money and Survival: The Proportional Relationship

Having enough money signifies you have the means to survive, which feels good and promotes a sense of self-confidence that is felt in other life areas as well. Without money, it is easy to slide into the destructive self-talk and sabotaging behavior patterns that reinforce your unworthiness to have more money. It is a vicious cycle, and, fortunately or unfortunately, the Universe brings you the vibrational match to what you are putting out. And THAT is the reason why that particular myth (the lack of personal worthiness to have money) has some credibility.

What is generally overlooked is that the energy came first and then the circumstance followed, instead of the other way around. When you decide to allow yourself to experience the feelings of self-confidence you have associated with money, money shows up because it is a match to your energy.

People's fears also lead them to believe that money is available in short supply, and that competition is required to "beat" people at having money (as in, if someone else has more, you won't have enough). A false sense of competition does not necessarily make you have more money, although it may make you stronger in some ways. Having the compulsion, drive or need to "be stronger" is based on a sense of not being strong enough, or the perception of weakness (regardless of truth). But even if you are strong and competitive, you could still find yourself without the wealth and financial resources you want.

One of the ways people address the fear of not having enough is to "save for a rainy day", which presumes one must have savings to be "ok". But it also doesn't define what a rainy day is, nor does it clarify how to protect from financial disaster, and it could even be creating the conditions for a financial tsunami (disaster) if that is the vibrational match for that person. If your energy is vibrating to bring a financial disaster, it will come able no matter the size of your nest egg—but the reverse is also true. By opening your perception to where you are vibrating financially, you allow yourself to consciously choose whether to have a financial disaster or not.

Essentially, money energy is very literal—it simply matches what holds the most intense energy in your space. If you have fears about money, you will receive opportunities to continue to fear money. If you buy into the collect (or hoard) money myths, you will receive experiences that prove them to be right and founded as well. If you are not attached to money fears and live in trust that you will be provided for, that is likely to be true as well.

Such money "growth" opportunities will show up over your lifetime in the form of teachers who will push you to consider your beliefs, because the Universe is an abundant Source in all ways. You are not here to exist on the fringes of poverty as a rule… but money is one of the key energy mastery curriculums here in Earth School. By understanding your money fears and the myths surrounding your socialization process, you give yourself the permission to go against them, play with them and discover a roadmap for your wealth evolution.

The Creative and Generative Energy of Money

We give money all kinds of power and energy and tend to ascribe to it all kinds of qualities, traits, and characteristics that we impose on it vs. being the truth. However, money is just money until we make it do something—then there is magic in money!

Think of electricity as an example of this generative force of money. Your house is connected to a huge source of energy that we call electricity, which is just waiting for you to flip the switch; however, the magic isn't in the electricity while in its unused state. It's only when you connect a device to that electricity which creates a result, like turning on an oven, air conditioner or light bulb, that the magic of electricity is revealed. The same is true with money and/or money energy—the magic is revealed in how it is used. Just like the electricity in your house, energy can power a torture chamber or an esteemed museum.

The energy of money is there—how are you going to choose to use and shape it?

Being centered in your inner security allows you to use your imagination, go beyond your comfort zone, transcend boundaries (of friends, expectations, social credibility, etc.) and evolve yourself and a solution which can express the generative force of money. Creativity requires a degree of innovation, a new way of connecting the dots and going beyond what already exists and THEN money can power up the next level of your endeavor.

One of the more interesting aspects of the generative energy of money is that you cannot create and be in fear at the same time. Many people will block the creative process if they don't feel the finances are available to support their creative output. But that puts the emphasis, and the pressure, on the least relevant part of the process… without the creative idea, money has no purpose. The constraint of money can actually inspire greater creativity.

In fact, if you don't take money too seriously, it's likely you will be able to see something through new eyes and the creativity will flow. THEN the money has a place to be attracted TO in your creative process and can initiate the generative power to bring your creativity to a tangible expression on the physical plane.

A ripple of creativity in new directions can lead to powerful expression. To power up the creative and generative force of money, let the energy start from within you… the money will be there as an effect of your creative energy.

How to Handle
Money Transitions

By definition, a transition is a time of change, when what 'was' is no more, and the 'what will be' has not arrived yet. It is a temporary state, but it offers a valuable opportunity to understand the nature of the change happening in your life and, therefore, your money. In fact, transitions are a necessary part of life to create your next best level, although they may feel uncomfortable when going through the shift.

There are two aspects to transitions, especially money transitions, you need to be aware of to be successful with money transitions. You will experience uncertainty in facing new responsibilities and choices, which, in turn, creates emotional turbulence if your security, stability, or safety is connecting to things related to the physical world instead of to Source energy.

It's an illusion that your financial choices today will affect your financial choices of the future. You have the ability to change your energy at any time and create a new reality.

You may find yourself in resistance to what's happening. When you hold on tightly to any situation, regardless of reasoning, you actually force it to change its state in a more dramatic way. That is, because the nature of life is dynamic change, when you close down the capacity of life to change and flow, you are stopping the flow of life. And the flow of money often parallels the life force energy of the people using it.

In terms of shutting down, or holding static your financial situation, you will do so for any number of reasons:

- you are afraid it will get worse (or better),
- you want to be loved as you are and if your money changes, your life will too,

- you don't know how to manage the changes that could occur,
- you don't have a plan on how to relate with your money in a new way,
- you want to stay in the same economic stratus as your friends,
- and exponentially more reasons that make sense only to you personally.

However, life is change so, consequentially, you will inevitably experience money transitions that are both self-directed and externally pressured. In either case, it's important you understand your priorities, your new resources and how to allocate them to get the end result you want (although that may change in the process of getting them!). Being able to go with the flow by consciously surrendering to the process will support you in releasing the energy you no longer want or need, as well as welcoming the new incoming money situation.

Remember to 'own' your money transition—you are the one creating it!!!

While there are tangible steps you can take throughout your money transition, including making sure your wants and needs are clearly sorted, pay attention to the energy behind the transition as the source of clarity and ease throughout your change process.

As you go through your money transition, look for your resistance points, or "hooks", because these limitations are the keys to the most effective and efficient path to get where you want to go. Limitations are the signposts, or curriculum of your personal Earth School, the Universe uses to lead you to your desired destination as quickly as possible (although not necessarily the most comfortably!).

By handling your energy as you go through the experience, you are addressing growth opportunities in a powerful way. For example, if you discover you have resentment, feel bitter, grumpy, cranky, or downright angry as a result of a money transition, this is a cue for you. Somewhere, on an energetic level, you've had anger that's unexpressed and which has been sending out a signal to invite scenarios that would make you express that anger, including this money transition. Consider this experience an invitation to get your anger resolved.

It may feel counter-intuitive to slow down to feel your energy in the midst of a major money transition, much less do the work to clear it, but this is what will make the transition as smooth as possible and ensure you don't need to experience another transition to get the same "growth opportunity". Why? Because what we resist, persists... that lesson will show up again and, next time, it will bring even more energy so you cannot avoid it. Since it's the energy that is creating the experience, addressing the energy directly is the quickest path to create change.

The Big Takeaway

Now that you are more aware of the triggers, limitations, co-dependency, and responsibilities of money, you have the keys to creating a new level of freedom in your relationship with money and possibly transition into a oneness with it.

To sum up the biggest concept presented in this section, when you have a sting, a ping, a 'charge', a reaction to _____, a weakness in making decisions, a resistance to _____, a sense of powerlessness, compromising yourself for money or any "symptom" that doesn't feel good when it comes to money, you are actively being invited to get to a new level of perception with your wealth.

Your expanded sense of awareness will seemingly magically draw into you new opportunities, relationships and situations that support your new wealth vibration, because you aren't being held back or tripped up by blocks that don't serve your money vibration. The Universe does not intend for you to be in poverty on any level and, when you really "get" that and get out of your own way, the Universe opens the floodgates of wealth in every way.

It may not be easy to handle all your money triggers and limitations, but most people find it exceedingly worthwhile after it's done.

7 Mistakes That Keep You from Making Money in Business As a Soul-Driven Entrepreneur

Who Are You?

As a visionary, forward-thinking, world-changing business owner, you are unique among traditional businesses. You are a world-changing business owner if you…

> … are driven to do your life's work as a business.
>
> … to leave your mark in the world by following your destiny.
>
> … make your unique contribution to the world through your personal gifts, skills, and knowledge.
>
> … risk taking what's important to you and expressing the essence of that to create a business.
>
> … hear your calling and have no choice other than to follow it.
>
> … use your life, through your business, to be of service.
>
> … are a pioneer, leading the way in creating innovative solutions for transformation.

Make a Bigger Difference Through Business

In this section, you will learn…

- The seven mistakes that sabotages many world-changing business owners,
- How not understanding each point can limit your success,
- How to move forward in your business in ways you likely haven't thought about before,

- The secret combination that creates your unique business success,

- And more.

There is no other time in the history of our country that opportunities are so prolific. As one of my mentors said, "Our greatest choice is in choosing which opportunities to pursue".

To make that choice as a world-changer, you must understand what will create success by your definition.

For me, becoming a world-changing entrepreneur is the accelerated path to personal development. Your business grows at the rate that you grow as a person; after all, your business is an expression of your true purpose. Makes sense, right?

Having worked with clients since 1998, I have the unique vantage point of seeing the greater "threads" and consequences of world changers not knowing how to create a business from the passions that compel them. And it's not really a choice for this emerging population—we who hear the call MUST go forward, whether we understand what we are doing or not!

The reason entrepreneurs are driven to seek support is because they are driven by this compelling need to express who they are to contribute to a better world. However, they are confronted by challenges they aren't quite able to handle cleanly and effectively, and which you might identify with as well.

It's likely you need some additional support, guidance, and fresh perspective if you:

… are in a state of consistent overwhelm with ideas, priorities, and lists.

… are not receiving enough income in a way that allows you to live comfortably (with the added insult that you are doing good work!).

… feel unsatisfied with the results of your business or life in general.

… live with an anxiety that can become crushing in the middle of the night.

… feel lost in your business (maybe life too).

… have lost touch with who you are and why you're doing what you're doing.

… feel alone and yet pulled in many different directions all the time.

Once you get the support and information you need, you'll be able to identify your blocks, obstacles, and tests to minimize or eliminate them. You'll feel positive momentum again and remember who you are in your true being. You'll begin to listen to, and trust, your own intuition as you build your world-changing business.

An Overview of the Seven Key Mistakes

Here are the seven key mistakes that sabotage many world-changing business owners—and how not knowing them could be limiting your business success.

Mistake	Effect	Action to Take
1. Lack of focus and clarity	Non-productive busywork	Clear sense of priorities and direction
2. Scarcity consciousness	Limitations throughout business	Abundant, confident mindset
3. Not having a business model	Wasted energy	Focused, strategic and practical plan to grow
4. Not seeing opportunities	Lost revenues or relationships	Stretch beyond where you are
5. Giving life to obstacles	Movement is slow or blocked	Increased energy flow
6. Not charging enough	Not making enough money	Own your gift and claim value
7. Knowing it all	Cannot receive new information	Have an open willingness

Mistake 1: Lack of Focus and Clarity

Most entrepreneurs understand the need for focus and clarity; however, they may get caught up in external definitions of each OR they forget what their original focus was intended to accomplish and allow their businesses / lives to run them. The "monkey mind" takes over and it's impossible to tune into the clarity of inner wisdom. The net result is busywork and, potentially, non-productive activities that aren't yielding the return they were hoping to achieve.

It's not that these people don't understand the basics of focus and clarity, because they do. Rather, it's that they are getting their checklist done very efficiently without necessarily being effective. This behavior this is addictive, in wanting to cross things off the list, and contagious, because one day will spill into the next when they didn't finish their "to-do" list, and they discover weeks slide by without having achieved what they planned for in the long run.

For example, one of my clients wanted to offer his first live event for approximately twenty people. He had lists, he was delegating responsibilities, he was getting up in the middle of the night to make sure he had checked his lists, and he was all over making this event happen. At the same time, he wasn't returning his messages to clients who wanted to schedule sessions, he wasn't taking care of his website (after 18 months, that project had made no progress), and had not found a facility for the aforementioned event. So he was busy and crossing his to-do list at the expense of achieving results. (Eventually, that "small" detail was resolved, the event went very well, and his website got underway again.)

Business success means having a clear sense of priorities and direction. Everything that doesn't contribute to your priorities and goals needs to fall away as it is less significant than this clarity of direction. Perseverance feels nearly effortless. You know what you're aiming for, clearly and specifically; as a result, you'll know when you've gotten there.

Mistake 2: Scarcity Consciousness

Throughout life, during socialization, you (and all humans) are "programmed" from childhood with beliefs, imprints, and attitudes that unconsciously become a part of the fabric of your being. How often have you heard "money doesn't grow on trees" or "there's not enough time to do that" or "you have to finish everything on your plate". It's insidious how we take in and internalize other's opinions that likely have nothing to do with our destiny. However, it becomes a reality that you, the business owner, must resolve because these unconscious paradigms affect your results.

Coming from a lack mindset will create challenges in your business for everything from not charging enough to not feeling like you have enough time to get everything done to not having the resources you need to not attracting enough clients or clients who don't have the money to afford your services.

A scarcity consciousness could also sabotage the outcomes of various situations; that is, you might expect a marketing initiative to give you a particular result and discover it's not that way at all. Mind you that's not a "failure"; in truth, it was an experiment that yielded an unanticipated outcome. Your awareness is what brings value to this situation because you can make new choices.

After a few of these types of situations and most people will begin to experience self-doubt—which becomes a reinforcement of the scarcity consciousness. "I'm not enough", "I don't know what I'm doing", etc. Then the entrepreneur feels maybe they don't know what they thought they did, so they aren't quite as capable as they thought in the beginning, and so, down goes their self-trust, and their business right with it.

At this point, people generally seek solutions outside of themselves because they clearly aren't able to generate the results they wanted. (Of course, that's only if their scarcity consciousness allows them to see beyond not having the resources to get this kind of support.)

As an example, a client hired me to help her understand why her freelance business wasn't working. She wanted to make a transition, wasn't sure how to make it, and her signals were mixed in asking for what she wanted because she didn't really know. She thought she wanted to move to northern California, so she and her husband bought a house and renovated it while they continued to not live in it and rent where they were at the time. They had no renters for their house for the first year but decided to rent it out after that as they weren't sure of their plans. They always made the mortgage but she lived every month in nervous anxiety they weren't going to make it, despite both of them being relatively successful in their respective businesses and not having the responsibilities of neither children nor debt.

We identified where some of her beliefs were no longer serving her, and she decided on a new business venture where she could be virtual. In creating her new business, she began to recreate her original issues with the "freelance" mentality until she saw how that limited her thinking. She realized she was holding her financial breath without good reason, and then discovered she could dream bigger instead of playing small and safe. In fact, she needed to go bigger to be the virtual entrepreneur she really wanted to be in the long run. Just two short years later, she successfully created her virtual business, positioned herself as an industry leader and had a client waiting list for her work!

The key here is to know the Universe has you covered, and that you have everything you need to create your successful world-changing business. You wouldn't be given a "mission by God" (to paraphrase the Blues Brothers) without also having access to everything you need to do it well.

Mistake 3: Not Having a Business Model

When entrepreneurs don't have some sort of plan, they are driving blind. They're forced to be reactive to what shows up as opposed to creating their business outcomes with intention. They don't know what's true for them (in this case that includes your business), they continue to ask themselves the same questions or find themselves in the same situations over and over again. They will take their cues from the people around them vs. following what they know for themselves from their own wisdom. And they miss opportunities because they are not positioned to see them, much less take advantage of them.

Having a plan means you know where you are going—it doesn't mean it's absolute, that there's no deviation, or that you even have to follow through with it. It's an exercise in the vibrational creation of what you want in your business for the benefit of your life's work. You can work through potential challenges without having to experience them. You can take what you have and go beyond with virtual innovation. You can share what you are doing with someone else so they "get it".

We world-changing business owners are ahead of the curve; that is, we are doing what we need to do but traditional business doesn't know how to help us pull it out of ourselves. However, when we finally understand our true calling, we can use the tools of traditional business to grow more quickly. Which, by the by, also includes setting up systems and processes that can take care of operations for you—but that's another subject.

Business success means allowing your business to have the foundation of a plan for strategic direction, timing, and credibility. One of the most effective signature systems I have developed over the years is to create a one-page business vision map. On one sheet of paper, literally map out how your business will progress through your offer, along with the increased support and deliverables, as well as associated revenues. It's a proven way to receive instant clarity on the "next best steps" to grow your business.

Making decisions and acting from your truths is as vital to your success as breathing is to fuel your life.

Mistake 4: Not Seeing Opportunities

There are times when we all are too busy to notice what's actually available to us; however, that can mean lost revenues to your business over time. It can mean you are not moving forward in flow with your business, which can lead to stagnant energy in your business. And if something isn't moving, growing, breathing… well, it's dying.

Not being able, or willing, to see new opportunities as they present in the moment—because you are so focused on doing what you do—can be deadly. Maybe you're attached to doing what you do because it's the only way you know how, or maybe it's because you don't know how to do the new thing that you just can't see it. Maybe you aren't thinking big enough to be able to take it in; instead, you could be focusing myopically on the details to avoid seeing the bigger picture, much like looking at the railroad tie and just not seeing the oncoming train.

While most enthusiastic world-changing business owners are taking calculated risks daily, sometimes they're missing the opportunities right at their feet. One of my clients had a mailing list of thousands, and yet, had never asked them to support her work directly by emailing them an offer. Another client decided to do more public speaking but passed on co-facilitating a workshop because it wasn't clearly a speaking gig. These may sound obvious but, to each person, they couldn't see their blind spot. (Fortunately, they were my clients at the time so they did get to pursue those opportunities.)

Opportunities are sometimes disguised as a teaching, a relationship, or an event. They also depend on timing, which I call "strategic synchronicity", much like driving on the highway. Strategic synchronicity is like when driving and you want to pass someone, you can jump over to go around or you can wait until the next "hole" to pass, right? The same holds true for opportunities—there will be more. However, each one holds its own special potential and can lead you to your next level.

The challenge is to stay connected to your purpose while you are stretching outside beyond where you are, to think bigger, to assess potential opportunities on a daily basis. Stop, look, and connect the dots in your world to see the ever-changing opportunities as they are created for you.

Mistake 5: Giving Life to Obstacles

What we focus on, expands. When we experience an obstacle that blocks our progress, our reaction to that determines our personal energy flow. If we continue to focus on the obstacle and what happened, re-tell the story throughout the day, add a little drama to the story, etc., we are actually giving life to the obstacle. It is now bigger than itself, and the net result is we are giving our energy away to this negative impediment. And movement is either slowed or blocked accordingly.

When obstacles are handled, minimized, eliminated, or removed by whatever means, they no longer need to have your life force energy. They are simply done. You, and / or the other involved parties, have gotten what you needed from that experience, and it's time to move on. That is positive energy flow.

When you are in positive energy flow, you will find you are more attractive to opportunities and people. You may find that synchronicity is a consistent occurrence for you. Obstacles, such as technology issues or conflicting projects or miscommunications or needing to be in two places at once or car problems (obviously, this list is nowhere NEAR complete for the average entrepreneur—there are TONS of obstacles out there…), are easily dealt with or avoided completely. It's about trust. When you know you are moving in the direction you need to go, and you trust yourself and the universe, you have no need to focus on the obstacles. They are merely testing you to make sure you know what you want or helping you see what isn't going to work to get you where you want to go.

Business success depends on experiencing increased energy flow in all ways. That is, when obstacles are minimized or eliminated, you feel good physically / emotionally / spiritually, and people / things / opportunities are attracted to you. There is a sense of optimism throughout your being and "things" just seem to line up in the best possible way for you. Focus on the possibilities rather than the challenges.

Mistake 6: Not Charging Enough

We world-changing entrepreneurial-types somehow don't own our gifts and claim our value consistently. Now sometimes the case is we haven't figured out the best way to package what we do in a way the world can recognize and reward us for financially. Sometimes we have a scarcity consciousness that doesn't allow us to see our value, ask for it, receive it, or even believe someone would actually pay us to do what we do/know/understand like breathing. We don't know we are special, that not everybody does what we do, or that it's important enough to charge for it.

When you aren't charging enough, you are violating the universal Law of Reciprocity; that is, you are not allowing the Universe to take care of you by receiving the measure of your value. And that's on you... you have to grow your ability to own your gifts and claim your value so you can package it in a way that other people can understand and value. If you don't value your service first, no one else will.

Consider the case of one of my clients who wanted to offer people comfort and hope during times of transition through mentoring, support, and inspiration. It was challenging to turn that into a business without compelling language or a concept, but even harder to generate revenue when she couldn't ask for her value from potential and current "clients" (using the term loosely). She was hard-pressed to write her bio, much less the benefits someone would receive in working with her, and nearly had apoplexy when considering her hourly rate would be $75 for such a personalized service (she'd never received that much money for her work before). She was basing her fees on what she thought her value was for her time, not the value of her service. She was also using historical parameters and then projecting that on and to her clients (and, since they couldn't afford to pay, she attracted a number of "pro-bono" clients). She was far more comfortable giving herself away to justify her importance to the extent that, when people offered to pay her, she didn't understand what they were saying—she literally couldn't hear them. Her phone call would drop, she could not understand they wanted to send her money, she had no idea what to say (as her credit card bills mounted in supporting her life). Over time, she has grown more comfortable (which is still relative) in charging consistently for her services (even if not yet all the way to her value!). It's a personal growth process to claim one's value, to be sure.

It can feel really vulnerable to offer your gift to the world, to do good work, and then not be paid for all your efforts. I've seen people slip into the victim role on that one—and it's vital to stay away from that. YOU are creating the experience you are having, so it's important to make sure you believe in your value first and foremost. The kicker is you have to determine what that value is, at least as a starting point, in order to even have a business.

Business success means making money, and to create a business that has real impact means your unique focus and intensity makes a contribution in a way that other people value and will pay to get it.

Mistake 7: Knowing It All

While it is important to have confidence and certainty about your business / life, it is also important to have an openness that allows good things to come into your world.

That is, an already full cup cannot hold more water. If you already know everything you think you need to know, you cannot receive new information. And new information is the lifeblood of growth in business and in life.

Business success means having an open willingness to receive, to learn, to become, and more. It means showing up with open arms to experience whatever is necessary in your success creation process. If you are unwilling or unable to do so, it is unlikely you will experience the fulfillment of creative fruition.

The Biggest Mistake of All

For one of my clients, after four years of trying to figure out how to make her business be successful (which meant knowing her niche/message/product, in measuring success/revenues/expenses, in marketing/delivering services/following up), she was fried. Her business wasn't working, she was frustrated and tired, she had tried taking classes and workshops but they didn't speak to her—they just added more to her to-do list and sense that she wasn't "enough" to get it all done. She found me and we started working together. That was when she realized the solution to her spinning world was simple.

The solution came down to doing what she could do, releasing what she couldn't and being responsible for what she did consciously decide to do. Rather than resisting what was happening, allowing her business to run her, or staying stuck in the "have to" mode, she took control of her business. She took stock of her "to do" list, and eliminated anything outdated, didn't apply or that she just didn't want to do. She prioritized what was left and scheduled it out with her plan. And she "owned" that she was where she was as a result of the decisions she'd made so far; after all, if she didn't own what she'd already created, she wasn't going to create a better future because she wouldn't be giving herself the power... she "got it".

As a visionary entrepreneur, you are used to multi-tasking, probably working long hours, having to handle the busywork AND the strategy of working ON your business and all of it usually takes more time than you think. In reality, once you slow down your internal speed and breathe, release what you don't need to do, be responsible for what you decide to do and "own" your business, your business will grow because the quality of your life just got better. You don't HAVE to do anything, really... this is about being YOU, with YOUR gifts, in YOUR contribution to the world, on YOUR personal transformation journey, through YOUR business.

In creating your business (or your life), there are three key indicators to know how to define your growth success.

1. You have to know where you want to go or end up.

2. You have to know where you are right now.

3. You have to determine the best way to get from where you are to where you want to go.

Note that "best" way does not mean shortest, most scenic, cheapest... it literally means YOUR best way. While there are many resources available to create change, each of them requires you DO something different. After all, when you keep doing what you've always done, you'll continue to get the same results.

When you are in alignment with your inner wisdom, your personal truths, and are centered in your personal BEING, you can create amazing results very quickly. It is the combination of being who you are and doing what is right for YOU that creates your business success.

Here's to accelerating your business success in changing the world by starting within.

Rewards Protect
Your Brain Chemistry

This is a concept that most people don't know about, much less talk about, in substantial terms.

While waiting for my doctor, I heard a DVD playing for background noise. Here are the three words caught my attention:

"Insufficient Reward Syndrome"

Say WHAT???

It's a real-world biological issue. I had no idea. The DVD that clanged this concept into my brain was referencing a biological neurotransmitter deficiency that prevents people from feeling happy. Naturally, I had to do a little more research.

The only resource I could find in non-medical speak was *"Behavior Therapy in Dealing with Depression"*. The idea is you can predict behavior based on positive reinforcement (or lack of it). Further, it said there are four factors that apply in a given behavior to positive reinforcement ratio. The four factors are as follows.

1. Frequency of positive rewards

2. Amount of positive rewards

3. The duration and continuation of the rewards once started

4. The amount of effort required to produce expected behavior

In other words, if your rewards are infrequent, too conservative and/or prone to stopping even though the behavioral demands continue, you're going to suffer Insufficient Rewards Syndrome.

Even more, if the effort to perform increases, the behavior to reinforcement ratio also increases and, if not met, also results in a deficient rewards syndrome state.

The bottom line is the quality of your life and health depends on your ability to reward yourself consistently in proportion to the effort you're putting out. It helps you to stay motivated and in joy.

Now, as an entrepreneur, chances are you're focusing on your bottom line rather than your body when you're deciding whether to give yourself a reward like time off, a new toy or a frivolous expenditure.

Rewards don't have to be expensive... but they are vital to your well-being. The teaching is you must work and play in proportion for your long-term healthy brain chemistry.

Because the cost of NOT giving yourself rewards as you go is far greater to your emotional, psychological, and biological health than the cost of the reward itself in time or money.

How to Claim Your Value
as a Business Owner

You know an entrepreneur who has claimed their value when you see them.

- They don't stutter when they state their fees.
- They have a vision for what's possible for their clients.
- Their attitude is expansive, accountable, and passionate.
- They know what they know without apology.
- They exude self-confidence and integrity.
- They have clarity of purpose.
- Their messaging is on point, relevant and interesting to their market.
- Their business, and how they conduct it, is congruent with their values.
- They think value vs. money.

And there are other cues… the idea is you consider the people who you know who have successfully claimed their value through their business to see their thoughts, behaviors, and decisions.

Obviously, knowing your value is vital to your business success. If you don't know why you are valuable, nobody else will either.

Claiming one's value in business can be a life-long journey for some people; as an entrepreneur, you must shorten that learning curve as quickly as possible in order to help more people and generate more revenues.

To that end, you will need to do some potentially intense self-discovery. The reality is that being a conscious entrepreneur requires a personal growth journey because your values, beliefs and limitations are revealed in your results; that is, you understand that you create your experience. Therefore, you can deliberately and intentionally accelerate your own development in order to grow your business.

Ask yourself (and answer) the following eight questions. There is no right or wrong—only what you need to know about yourself and your value through your business.

1. In what way do I feel unique to any other person (including industry colleagues)?

2. What distinctive benefit(s) do my clients receive from me through my business?

3. While what I offer may be similar to another solution available on the market, how do I do it differently?

4. If someone offered a lump sum figure for what I bring to my clients, and it was the ONLY amount of money I could receive for the rest of my life, how much would I ask for?

5. If money were no object and I could do anything I desired, what business would I choose to be in and why?

6. What would you need to believe about who you are to claim and embody your value financially through your work?

7. If you didn't worry about judgment or market conditions, what is the first number that leaps to mind about what you should be charging? (If it's different than what you're charging now, your task is to close that gap.)

8. Make a list of 25 benefits your clients receive from you. Then go deeper into each one to list the REAL benefit of each one. (For example, personal transformation could be about inner life serenity for your clients.)

Consider your list to reduce it to the top 10 real benefits and match those with your products and services. Then match your current fees with the real benefits… are they commensurate or do you need to raise your prices (as you will likely find)? As in, what's the value of inner life serenity for someone who was in painful patterns or looping negative self-talk?

If, as a result of these questions, you find you surface deep-seated limitations, constrictions or shadow beliefs, congratulations—that's the point. When you find them, you give yourself conscious choice about whether to allow them to continue dictating your value in business (and life).

On the other hand, if you discover helpful insights, turn them into an action plan and get them into your daily routine as soon as possible. All the insights in the world are meaningless if you do not act on them.

Defining Your
Prosperity Path:
How to Make Opportunities
(And a Living!)
From Your Wisdom

Context:
The Energy Economy

We have entered an age like none known before… I call it the Energy Economy.

Scientists have long known that everything is made of energy; the rest of us have finally figured out form follows energy. That is, you cannot have something manifest physically unless it existed in energetic form first.

Your thoughts are an energy form—one of the most powerful, in fact. Your intentions, interpretations of life's experiences and emotional expression are energy forms. Your state of being, relationships, and self-worth are energy forms.

All of it, with your attention, becomes wisdom.

For the first time in history, people with wisdom are not only respected more deeply than the average civilian but they are respected enough to be paid for their wisdom. Perspective is the most valuable thing you can offer another person because they cannot see what you do; instead, they can only see what they are familiar with and allow themselves to see.

Others recognize the value of leveraging life lessons based on wisdom rather than living them personally, allowing them to focus on the good stuff without experimenting and, potentially, becoming distracted or paying an unnecessary toll of time, energy, and resources.

When you are called to be a Wisdom Worker in this Energy Economy, it's likely you:

- Seem to 'know' things before others do (IF they ever do).
- Feel compelled to share or even teach what you know.
- Find your life has had (seemingly) more challenges than others in superficial comparison.

- Feel 'connected' in ways that others don't appear to be by their words or actions.
- Are a high communicator and, possibly, an adopter of digital ways to engage with people.
- Have had people tell you you're an 'old soul'.
- Try to blend in with others but still 'stick out' enough that people seek your counsel (in strange places—parks, parties, the gym, etc.).
- Have had strangers share details with you they've not even breathed to their best friend.
- See life with metaphysical eyes—you know that "messages" and guidance surrounds us.

You will help guide people to their evolution to reach their next best level. That individual growth (ideally, progression) is what will form our collective future.

And so, you can see we all (those you know and those you have yet to meet) need you to define your prosperity path so you can be abundant and, therefore, have more to share with the rest of us. As you impact just one person at a time, you change their world, which changes the world for those they love, care about and connect with, which changes the next person's world… you are creating the future by sharing your wisdom now.

Challenges of Wisdom-Based Business

Here's the thing… just because you have wisdom doesn't mean you know how to make a living from it. Maybe you're not comfortable talking about yourself. Maybe you want to just put your head down and work. Maybe you can't figure out how to do what you do if you aren't physically working with someone and/or fear technology and the digital world. Maybe you don't have a business model that can produce consistent revenue. Maybe you're intimidated (or even afraid of!) the dreaded "SALES" you have to do to be in business.

At the same time, you're committed to sharing your wisdom because you know the difference it can make for others. You love serving people! Maybe you've even made some money at it but you know you can (and need to / should) make more. So you're committed to doing what it takes to follow your calling as a wisdom worker into becoming an entrepreneur so you can get paid to share what you know.

The good news is it's actually not hard to make money from your wisdom. In fact, once you understand the strategy of it, you will see how you can progress your clients through greater levels of value in your work in a way that serves both of you.

A quick note: if you are called to the entrepreneurial path, it's likely you've got what's called the 'bright shiny object syndrome'. That means you want to do this, and this, and oh—there's that too! It can be overwhelming to try to round up all your knowledge, expertise, and talent to all focus in the same direction. And yet, that's exactly what needs to happen. The good news is you're reading this now to learn the truth about opportunities, your wisdom and how to present them in a progressed business model as your path to prosperity.

Opportunities for Wisdom-Based Business

Our purpose here is to create a formula for making a living based on your wisdom and opportunities. Let's begin by exploring opportunities.

Despite the title of this section, you don't actually need to *make* opportunities -because they are everywhere! Instead, it's about developing discernment in determining which ones are the best to pursue.

Think of it like trying to choose a movie from the plethora of options, both in titles and in platforms—DVR? Amazon? Netflix? Hulu? How do you know what to watch? Which one is the best for you? What happens if you don't watch one or choose one that you don't really like but you feel you have to watch it until the end anyway? Will it come on again? Can you watch it for free now but have to pay for it later?

In business, how do you know your best revenue model? What if you don't know something? What if you commit to one strategy and discover another one is better? Where should you advertise? Who should you work with to help you? What will your ideal future clients respond to when you put yourself out there so they become a paying client?

Your inner wisdom helps you to make such decisions on a routine basis. You identify which opportunities to take and which to pass based on current conditions. That is true of any other opportunity in life and/or business. An opportunity is an opening to get to your next place of being. Often an opportunity involves some degree of growth to be able to take advantage of and/or sustain it.

If you have a karmic agreement to grow in a particular area, you will have continuous opportunities appear over your lifetime to help you learn what you need for your next level. Once you "get" whatever it is that you needed to learn, you graduate to your next set of opportunities.

But you know this... it's part of the wisdom that you're actually here to teach.

Three Ways to Identify a Good Opportunity

To help clarify this teaching, following are three ways to determine a good opportunity.

1. The growth / benefit potential exceeds the required input.

If you can see the reward is positive in the end despite the effort and whatever else is needed for you to take advantage of the opportunity, chances are it's a good one for you.

If the magnitude of what is required from you is daunting or overwhelming, but you have even a glimmer of something better as a result of the opportunity, it's worth taking the risk.

After all, it's about experiencing the range of your personal possibilities for your best growth AND adding to your 'wisdom bank' to benefit others over time.

2. It keeps showing up for you.

If it seems the same types of opportunities keep presenting, such as you are attracting the same difficult client with a different name or your energy fades out at the same time of day or your money issues don't change over time, these are patterns of opportunities that are inviting you to get to your next level. (The only thing worse than this type of opportunity showing up is NOT having it show up for you—or not being able to see it to move forward in a bigger way!)

When you see a pattern to your opportunities, it's time to do something different—take advantage of it and see where it takes you!

3. You will regret not taking it.

There are times when you may not know an opportunity is the right one or at the right time, but you can feel you would experience loss, sadness or regret if you don't take advantage of it when it's right there.

Sometimes it comes down to a split decision in the moment—that is your spirit demanding you show up for yourself beyond your comfort zone and in trust that you will have the experience and outcomes needed for your best and highest good.

Ideally, at any point in life, you can look at where you are and where you've been without regret. In my humble opinion, suffering is at least partially attributable to missed opportunities. We see them in hindsight or we are bound by some external "thing" (people's opinions, perceptions of our own lack of resources or whatever) to not see them or not take advantage of them when they show up.

The only solace you can take from that awareness is you will get another chance if it is truly your opportunity. It will come again, maybe in different form and at another time but, once you see it on any level, you can know it as your next best opportunity.

Now let's bring all that down to a business level. As an entrepreneur (someone who is offering a valuable deliverable to solve a problem or meet a need in exchange for money), you need to determine which opportunities will benefit you and your business the most.

In business, a good opportunity:

- Teaches you something you must have for knowledge or experience.
- Brings you one step closer to your goals.
- Generates a return greater than the input(s) required to activate it.

Wisdom Is Creative Energy That Shapes Form

Now that you have context for why your wisdom work is so important, and you understand you must choose your opportunities as steppingstones to your next best level, it's time to explore a bit about your wisdom. Then we'll put it all together to show you how to make a living from it.

Contrary to what most people think, wisdom is NOT an accumulation of information, data, or facts. Instead, wisdom IS a state of being, a presence, a way of interpreting the world around you. It's a feeling people get when they connect to you either physically or through your words, images, videos, and social media presence.

Take a moment to consider the people you deem wise. It's likely there's a sense of being grounded, of being compassionate, of security and appreciation for life, regardless of their profession or specialty. Often these are people who have suffered in some way. Age, gender, physical appearance... none of these things can tell you about the degree of wisdom that person holds; instead, it's how they communicate through their energy and their words.

Chances are, by now, others have reflected to you that you have wisdom. It may be honed on a specific life area, or for a particular audience, or to help others achieve a particular result. The key to your wisdom is how comfortable you are in embodying it, as that is what creates your state of being. Your state of being is what creates your 'station', or status, in life.

In other words, when you embody, share, and teach wisdom, you are creating an energy that, eventually, manifests on the physical plane in some way. That will either be something for you (material possessions, a vacation, cash flow, etc.) and/or it will be something for someone else (your client's transformation, insight or paradigm shift that results in a different material world).

Either way, form *will* follow energy. Your wisdom is that energy.

Find Your Prosperity Path Through Ease

The way to prosperity for you is through doing the thing that comes the easiest to you. That is, if you're a writer, write. If you're a talker, talk. If you're a teacher, teach. The modality with which you are most comfortable will be your smoothest path for creating prosperity from your wisdom.

That said, following is a chart with several business models you may want to consider in creating a living from your wisdom. Know you may find yourself drawn to more than one and/or see where they could combine to support you in making a comfortable living. Notice how each of the offers builds off the one previous to it for access to you, depth of value to your client(s) and for potential revenues.

Your personal path to prosperity arises naturally from your primary communication preference combined with strategy to deliver value to your ideal clients.

Modality	Strengths	Venues	Progressed Business Model
Writer	Uses language and combines words to create compelling action	Book/e-book, reports, guides, email, video scripts, blog	1. Book 2. Autoresponder series for how-to 3. Video product (can be outsourced) 4. Membership site
Teacher	Makes complex concepts attainable	Classes, workshops, seminars, retreats	1. Initial class (tele-/in-person) 2. 4-part class series 3. Workshop 4. Retreat
Speaker	Reaches large numbers of people	Keynote, break-out, speaker bureaus	1. Book (can be outsourced) 2. Speaking gigs 3. Telesummit 4. Video product
Actor	Performer who can handle spotlight	Live events, video, stage	1. Intro video series 2. Speak from the stage 3. Workshop 4. Retreat
Coach	Observer who asks the right questions	Phone, Skype, in-person 1:1 or small groups	1. Intro Teleclass 2. 4-part webinar series 3. Breakthrough session 4. Coaching package

Modality	Strengths	Venues	Progressed Business Model
Mentor	Been there, done that	Phone, Skype, in-person 1:1 or small groups	1. Intro Video 2. Self-Assessment 3. 1:1 Breakthrough session 4. Mentoring program
Reader	Sees patterns and describes them	Phone, Skype, in-person 1:1 or small groups	1. Authority blog 2. Local appearances 3. 1:1 session 4. Group classes
Healer	Can hold space with pain	Phone, Skype, in-person 1:1, group sessions	1. 1:1 sessions 2. Video product 3. Group classes 4. Book
Artist	Translates abstract through creative expression	Physical products, live events, workshops	1. Individual products + interpretation 2. How-to appearances at live events 3. Video product 4. Membership site

Identify Your Ideal Clients

Amazingly, one of the best ways to identify your ideal clients is to look in the mirror. That is, think back to where you were when you had the issue, problem, concern or challenge you now know how to solve—the one you are packaging into a solution. Who were you then? What did you think about? What words would you have used to describe your situation? If you considered investing in a solution then, what was the tipping point for your decision?

Once you understand yourself, then consider who is buying your solutions now. Look for the commonalities that can become traits or qualities that define your ideal clients.

Then consider who you WANT to work with as an ideal client. Do these qualities, traits and/or characteristics all add up to give you a persona of your ideal client? Is that persona someone who is looking for what you offer? Can that persona afford to pay for it? Can you find that type of person easily in the marketplace so your marketing is effective?

In the end, being a successful business owner means offering and delivering a solution that people want, are looking for and are willing to pay for... through your ideal clients, the Universe rewards you for being on your right prosperity path.

Let's explore next how to find your personal formula for prosperity and claim your money magic.

Finding Your Formula: Discover the Keys to Claiming Your Money Magic

Setting Expectations
Around Your Money Magic

This section is designed to help you understand how to claim your money magic by understanding and consciously using your own personal wealth manifestation process. We will explore the roles of your own self-nurturing, illuminating and then living according to your unique purpose, the big money formula and practical action steps to take in claiming your money magic.

Please understand the following are ways which can open you to receiving and shifting your energy, but they aren't "truths". That is, they will only work if you are open to and use them, but there is no harm done if you don't. Think of these keys as "tools" that need to fit the job you want them to do—if you want to hang a picture, you don't usually use a monkey wrench, right? Feel free to use the energy tools you are drawn to and leave the rest without guilt or negative side effects (since they are not resonating with you).

A note for expectations management: teaching you how to claim your money magic and then expecting big changes immediately isn't the point here. This is about supporting you in working with Source energy proactively and deliberately for your personal wealth manifestation process. It's intended to be an introduction to a real-world, sustainable ways to work with the energy that permeates all of your life and physically anchors your energetic manifestation process. Big money is always waiting for you, so it is more a matter of letting go of the energy blocks that are resisting it, which will allow money to flow into your life, instead of you desperately chasing the money.

The keys to wealth contained in this section (and the rest of this book) are designed to work with both your right / intuitive and left / linear brain; both sides of your brain offer valuable resources to any creation process. By using all the resources and energy available to you, you can create more of what you want in your life—including money!

As you work through this material, take the time to consider your own thoughts on each section before moving to the next; the purpose is to allow you to establish your "baseline" process before you are influenced by the information you read. After you've read the information, you'll naturally have new insights; at that point, go back to your original thoughts and pull out the key elements of your personal money formula so you can build on them as you read further. By the end of this section, you should have a new awareness of how you can claim your money magic.

The Money Magic Formula

A formula, by definition, is a set order of methods to reproduce definable results. It is a proven system that orders certain variables and creates a known or expected outcome (think recipe of ingredients that creates a delicious outcome). And when you follow a sound, solid formula, there are certain steps you take to get the results you want. So wouldn't it be so much easier to just have the money magic formula to create money?

Without further ado, here is The Money Magic Formula.

$$\frac{\text{Perception x Your Choices x Action Taken}}{\text{Resistance to Change}} = \text{Outcome (Money)}$$

Let's take the formula in order of appearance... first up is Perception.

Perception

According to Wikipedia, the definition of perception is: 1) the process of attaining awareness or understanding of sensory information, and/or 2) receiving, collecting, and the action of taking possession / apprehension with the mind or senses.

By expanding your perception, you are expanding your ability to take in information on a number of levels (sensory, visually, spiritually, etc.) which enhances your ability to make informed decisions from a more holistic perspective. Cultivating perception is one of the key methods to self-development and, some would say, enlightenment because perception underlies anything you learn or experience in life.

There are various scientific theories about the development of perception; two of the most significant for our purposes here are the Piagetian theory, which states there is no understanding of perception without experience, and the Ecological theory, which suggests the environment provides information for direct perception. In either case, the process of perceptual learning means you are increasing your efficiency in responding to stimuli as well as enhancing your discernment in assessing situations and making decisions.

There are an exponential number of methods you can use to develop your perception so it's important to follow your own intuition as to what makes the most sense for you. In the spirit of expanding your perception as a way to experience life conditions more consciously and completely, particularly with regard to your relationship with money, the following are five suggestions for ways you can develop your perception. Whatever has a sting, a ping or a charge has a negative power for you to meditate on further.

Five Awareness Practices

1. Pay attention to your actions and behaviors where money is involved; even more, notice your thoughts and feelings when making purchasing and investment decisions.

2. Notice your motivations around giving, donating, or tithing money.

3. Become aware of your potential projections toward people who appear to have a lot of money—and those who don't.

4. Consider whether you judge people for their apparent economic status and/or how they choose to allocate their financial resources.

5. Monitor your self-talk to determine what it is really saying and if it is supportive or sabotaging for you when it comes to handling your money.

The above is a short list. The idea is you start becoming aware of what's happening with, around and within you in terms of money. One important caveat... do not believe any of the thoughts and/or judgments from the above exercise as real or true. Simply notice you are experiencing them and take note of the one(s) that seem so real you want to buy it (them) hook, line, and sinker.

The goal is you enhance your ability to perceive what's happening in the moment as it happens, as opposed to reacting due to unconscious projections, conditioned thinking, or self-sabotaging behavior.

Now let's consider the invitation for growth as referenced by the simple world 'choice'.

Your Choices Generate New Possibilities

Choices are your ability to generate options by seeing the possibilities (even in the challenges) and then choose your next best direction from them.

Choices can be simple or complex, depending on the number of variables involved and the perceived significance of the potential consequences to be experienced post-choice. Most people like having choices because there is a sense of perceived freedom inherent in being able to have options from which to choose. Likewise, when a choice feels constricted or limited somehow, the outcome may feel lackluster, or not quite fulfilling.

In every moment, you are choosing to manage your energy—you can "buy" an emotion as real (and experience all which that means) or not (simply releasing it without getting unconsciously "hooked" by it). You can choose to see the wonder and the beauty in any situation (emotion, relationship, issue, etc.) rather than getting caught up in the "negative", or shadow, of it. Remember you are always choosing to have the experience, whatever the reason. When the reason is unconscious, therein lies the disconnect. You may not even be aware of your unconscious payoffs of a particular choice.

For example, one of my clients consistently found herself in jobs where her talents were marginalized and her pay was too low for her skills. Once she discovered that she was replaying her mother's perception of her, and her mother's pay scale for what she should be paid, she no longer had to take jobs that proved her mother right. She now has a career that pays commensurate with her contributions.

Having a 'shadow' experience through your choices, conscious or not, are part of your personal growth journey. As such, you can choose to see the magic in what you are creating instead of despairing about it. Make it your quest to make lemonade from the lemons you grew and chose to harvest from your virtual lemon grove. Your choice, ultimately, is to see the illusion in what's happening and shape it to the experience you want to have in each moment.

What gets really interesting about choices is having unlimited choices. In this case, people might feel confused and/or destabilized with too many options. Or they might feel indifferent because they don't have a structure by which to approach making the choice. Or they might regret the alternatives they didn't choose.

The person choosing might also think (which is a misidentification) they get to control the outcome of their choice simply because they chose it from among their many options (like, they picked a winner in some way—for example, after choosing a restaurant and expecting / demanding it be an amazing experience). That person might also think the outcome of their choice reflects on who they are as a good (or not) person, which is not true. Choice is merely something we get to do—opportunities are presented to get us what we want on a vibrational level.

That distinction becomes apparent only through perception and choosing what to change, because different perceptions will cause different opportunities to show up.

There are various ways you can, and probably do, use to make a choice. For example, you might weigh the options by balancing the importance of one choice against another (comparing them with a pro and con list) or among many different options (with a grid analysis to account for multiple factors) or phoning a friend for an opinion, as examples.

You might consider the pressure(s) that are for and against the change, forecast the possible consequences, invite input from trusted advisors, ask yourself questions about the choice to be made (to invite new potentialities), brainstorm possibilities around the choice and / or options, do a cost / benefit analysis to look at potential financial outcomes, create an if / then flow chart or even do a mind map to create a visual representation of the relationships of the possibilities and potential outcomes.

No matter the system you use, remember to come back to this—it is just a choice and you have the freedom to make it any way you want. Your freedom comes when you can make choices simply because you want to make a choice—no right, no wrong, just your will making it.

Six Thinking Hats for Making Choices

Edward de Bono, in his book Six Thinking Hats, offers a way to organize your thinking in six different ways, which may be another helpful approach to take in any given choice situation. Following is a quick reference list of the 'six hats' of thinking and considering your choice from various perspectives:

1. White Hat: This type of thinking focuses on the available data, looking at information (or gaps in information), trend analysis and using historical data for considering new options.

2. Red Hat: This type of thinking uses intuition, hunches, emotion and gut instincts to consider options; there is less reliance on understanding linear reasoning and more

emphasis on the emotional response from yourself and the people potentially affected by the choice / options / outcome(s).

3. Black Hat: This type of thinking uses pessimism in a positive way; that is, consider why something won't work because this helps to illuminate the weak points for any particular choice (so you can minimize / eliminate / be prepared for problems / start over with less risk and more quickly and easily).

4. Yellow Hat: This type of thinking comes from optimistic consideration of your choice and the options; this is where you see all the benefits of making the choice, the value of the choice-making process and options, and motivates you to keep going in the face of challenges that may make your choice seem difficult.

5. Green Hat: This type of thinking is all about creativity, innovating on the fly, keeping all options open as possibilities, and following them wherever they may lead in generating new ideas, solutions, and possibilities.

6. Blue Hat: This type of thinking is all about controlling the choice process, so the focus is on being the "traffic cop" of using the various hats at various points in the choice-making process.

Regardless of what 'hat', or choice consideration, method you use, you are increasing your perception around the choice, your options, the potential consequences, and the energy around the choice point in which you find yourself.

In fact, there are usually many more choices than you might realize at first glance. Notice from a small subset of choices comes an unending supply of choice based on your point of view. For example, if you are a cashier, taking money from customers is purely transactional; however, when you are the customer in that relationship, that money is leaving your bank account. Same money—but completely different perspective.

Altogether, you are the inventor of your choices and, as such, you are always free to make a new choice when the one you made previously no longer serves.

Moving on... let's consider 'Action' as a part of the *Money Magic Formula*.

Actions to Work Your Money Magic

Action is the movement or physical action you choose to take as a result of your intention, whether conscious or not. The action happens because you physically do something with what you know. It is what you end up doing / being / thinking in the end of a situation. For example, if you want to be fit and you end up watching movies while eating ice cream, the action you took in this formula would be you became a couch potato. (It's not right or wrong, just the way you chose to handle it at that moment). Action is the final thing you did in any given situation or circumstance.

After the fact, it's important for you to consider how you showed up in that situation as a significant key to knowing where you are in your personal power. Once you know that, you can see how you are showing up in the moment to give yourself freedom of choice in the present.

Most situations in life are not permanent, because life is dynamic. You are not meant to stay stuck in one place—challenging situations are simply invitations and / or opportunities to grow to your next best level. If you find your actions are not what you want them to be, there are most likely energetic blocks in the way. (So you CAN be fit if that's really what you want!)

YOU are at choice on how and when to grow to your next best

level. By "owning" what occurred in your action(s), taking responsibility for it and recognizing you created it, you acknowledge what you've already created through your choices, which will empower you to consciously create what you want in your future with clarity and intention.

Which brings us to the last component of the Money Magic Formula… resistance to change.

Your Resistance to Change Blocks Your Money

You would likely agree it's hard to receive a hug with your arms folded across your chest; the same is true for Source to bring you money when you are in resistance to receiving the experiences which are a part of the wealth cycle.

Through your desire to attract, invite, generate, welcome and enjoy a new relationship with money, you are asking for something you've never had before… and the only way to actually experience that is to be open to what you've not had before. This new experience will naturally feel unfamiliar—the 'hook' is to not label it as wrong or bad when it's different (which it must be) from what it was in the past.

As humans, we have the habit of continually doing the familiar, whether it is positive or not for us, simply because it's familiar, comfortable and, therefore, perceived as stable and safe (whether or not it actually is).

There's a fable about a frog that jumps into a pot of water; what he doesn't know is it's sitting on top of a burning stove so the water will boil. As the water heats up, he's so busy doing the backstroke and enjoying the water he doesn't realize the water is becoming hot; instead, his body simply adjusts to the rising temperature. He never jumps out, so we can surmise what happens to him; he stayed where he was thinking he was safe as he mentally accommodated the boiling temperatures. In what area of life are you doing the same? Where are you resisting change, particularly with regard to your relationship with money?

Based on your own life experience, you've probably noticed there is a varying degree of discomfort when you have created anything new in your life, both in the transition and as you got used to the new thing or state of being. It is scary to go beyond your comfort zone into something you aren't quite certain about and that can alert your internal protection systems to go into overdrive.

That internal security mechanism seeks to consolidate for protection and maintenance until the new information can be thoroughly assessed and assimilated. Why? Because stability, safety and security are core human needs. Faith can transcend this base protection mechanism; however, your inner biology will always seek that comfort zone.

Since the physical world is fundamentally oriented around constant change, a person never truly gets safety, security, and stability when it is attached to the physical. By cultivating your personal development, you know your true source of support is within. There is nothing external that can give you the sense of being grounded and safe like your own internal connection to Source energy. When you are really dialed into Source as your stability, you can be completely open to the new experiences for which you are asking without fear.

In fact, your strength is in your vulnerability; that is, as vulnerable as you may seem, it is vulnerability that has no shields, defenses, or barriers to what is coming into your experience. Your arms are open to receiving. On the surface, that can seem unprotected; however, when you are secure in trusting and knowing Source has you covered, you have no need to put up false barriers (even if they are motivated by a positive intention to care for yourself).

As Source is giving you messages, it's vital to be open to receiving them AND to taking action based on what you learn. Some of them may present challenges, like moving to a new state to take advantage of new opportunities, but when you can see the magic in the message, it makes it a lot easier to follow through on them.

Remember you are co-creating with Source energy. By feeling into what you want, you are deliberately aligning your energy with Source. Take the time to consider whether you want something completely different or a different form of something you already have (or had) in your life. Where do you feel the need to grow? And if you feel a sting, a ping or a 'charge' when the answer comes to you, there is a "hook", or limitation, asking for your attention so it can be addressed and released.

By being open to experiences without resistance to change, you are allowing yourself to receive without restriction, which is highly attractive for money (and a whole lot of other good things!).

Putting It All Together

A quick reminder of the Money Magic Formula (and it's likely you will resonate differently with the formula after reading this information).

$$\frac{\text{Perception x Your Choices x Action Taken}}{\text{Resistance to Change}} = \text{Outcome (Money)}$$

Altogether, your expanded perception plus your conscious choice and the actions you take (both physically and energetically) is the top half of the Money Magic Formula. All these concepts are divided by your resistance to change. When your resistance to change is significant, your perception, choices, and actions will have a very limited effect on your outcome. Conversely, lesser resistance gives more power to, or amplifies, your perception, choices, and actions to create your desired outcome.

Next, we'll explore the Three Keys to Wealth that are essential to claiming your money magic.

The Three Keys to Wealth

In claiming your money magic, you can use three vital keys to access your wealth more fully and more easily. Just like the denominations of money (a penny to nickel to dime to quarter to dollar, etc.), each of them builds on and relates to the others—there is no true "end" to the Three Keys. Using the Three Keys organizes your energy, albeit in a somewhat linear way, so you experience a continuous, dynamic oneness with your wealth.

As with the Money Magic Formula, the Three Keys will likely appear to be common sense, but that is the exactly the mystery of any masterpiece… it is divinely simple. True mastery simply is.

The Three Keys to Wealth (read from the bottom up) are as follows:

Personal Manifestation Process
Illumination of Purpose
Self-Nurturing

Self-Nurturing

Let's start with the end on this one… your personal energy is your currency.

You may have noticed the play on words there. Currency is, of course, the flow of your dynamic state of being AND, in this case, it's also the key to your money.

Giving to yourself first allows you to be 'full'. Not only is that a state of abundance in your being, it's also necessary to be full so you can give to others. Abundance is your vibrational emanation. (That is a fancy way to say you glow with energy that others can feel, either positive or negative, either abundant or scarcity oriented.)

Think about it… if your needs aren't met, you are (by definition) operating at a deficit. How can you possibly have something (anything, much less something of quality) to give to someone else to help meet their needs? Self-care means making you your own biggest priority.

When traveling by plane, the crew advises to put your own oxygen mask on first in case of trouble and then assist others with theirs—it doesn't work the other way around because if you become incapacitated, who is going to help you? You both would be in trouble if you didn't take care of yourself first. The same is true for your self-care. Your Being will seek to take care of your physical needs first when you are compromised (ill, injured, stressed, fatigued); it has to so you have energy for enjoying your wealthiest life.

Filling yourself up first is something that takes less time than you probably think it does, because it can happen on multiple levels at the same time and it can yield significant results. Take a moment to recall the last time you felt really refreshed and enlivened after a great meal… it was probably a tasty meal, being in the company of good friends and people you care about, in a nice environment with appropriate lighting and music with attractive dishes and a table centerpiece… you get the idea.

The refreshed vitality you enjoyed came as a result of filling up on multiple layers—sensory, tactile, emotional, physical, psychologically, energetically, in an ambient environment—and that is a great way to approach your own "fill-up" experience.

Your self-fulfilling experience is in your hands. Giving to yourself is the gift you then give to the world.

So why don't people nurture and fill themselves up first? There are too many reasons to get into here—entire libraries are filled with books on the subject!

However, generally speaking, all those reasons can be distilled into one (or more) of the following four categories.

1. Lack of knowledge (they don't know how or feel they need special skills)

2. Habits (they are living on autopilot and not unconscious to how little that take care of themselves; like a martyr, they think they are suffering for someone else's benefit)

3. Permission to receiving (or, not receiving nurturing as they are unwilling or unable in some way to receive for themselves)

4. Environment (indulging in physically, emotionally, energetically destructive surroundings)

These categories can be further consolidated into unconscious energies, running by default under the surface. Among them are: anger (being in resistance or rebellion as a result of personal boundaries being dishonored), fear (a lack of feeling safe or being judged as selfish in making themselves a priority), or lack of self-worth (self-esteem, self-confidence, self-respect, self-affinity) which will effectively prevent someone from considering themselves a priority and taking action to support that.

You are here as a physical representation of divine energy; nurturing yourself means taking care of precious divine energy in tangible form. That happens on all levels—physically, energetically, psychically, intellectually, sexually, emotionally, and spiritually. Granted, that's a lot of levels, but you are an amazing being! By balancing the fulfillment needs of your body(ies), you keep your life interesting, honor your reason for being, and stay present with your needs as they change.

Filling up looks different for each person; in fact, your needs will change over time as well.

Developing your own self-nurturing means looking at how you choose to own and interpret your life's events. To what degree you are willing to show up for yourself and stand powerfully for who you are? Are you willing to receive the nurturing that comes from the Universe through you and the people in your world as messengers of the divine? When you are glowing from healthy self-nurturing, you radiate wellness, confidence, AND abundance... not to mention, you just feel good.

Illumination of Purpose

Another Key to Wealth is the illumination of your life purpose. When you are aligned with your unique reason for being, the Universe is positioned to reward you—there is a clear and open "oneness" with the Universe around your illuminated purpose.

There is really only one purpose each of us has, and that is to get closer to Source energy. You are the physical representation of divine energy and, accordingly, there is a part of your soul that remembers the connection with pure Source energy and yearns to reclaim that experience.

Since you are a piece of Source energy, your "job" is to have a physical experience and give that experience back to the greater consciousness in totality, regardless of what the actual experience is (positive or not, expansive or not, etc.). You elect what kind of experience you are going to have and then make decisions to create it. The power, and responsibility, to create your purposeful life is yours— you are the only one who chooses (or even CAN choose) the quality of it.

While in physical form, your purpose is to have "oneness" with Source energy; the path you take to get there is uniquely yours. You are always in the position of exercising free will in making choices that support the expression of your individual gifts.

Let's take a moment to consider what your purpose is not... it is not any of the following.

- A job
- The next big "click"
- Dependent on other people
- Found outside of you
- Something that feels forced to do
- Dependent on learned skills
- Something someone else can do the way you would do it
- Something you have to wait to experience

Your purpose is always present in some form throughout your life, independent of situations, relationships, or circumstances. It is always seeking to express in some way because that is why you are here.

For example, take a moment to consider the "threads" of your life, which are those commonalities you experience with different people / situations at different times of your life. You might recall hearing people say "oh, I always feel so _____ after we hang out", or "you're always so _____" or "it seems like you are always up to _____"— these types of statements are echoing a consistency in your life that become a "thread" of your purpose.

While you might have a desk job in a cubicle, people might tell you they always feel so much better when you're around, or you might be writing your novel when you have time "on the side" and you find people saying you're so well-organized with your time— these are examples of your "threads" showing up. You are doing one thing but the validation you get comes from a seemingly unexpected place about something you find very natural.

Your purpose is always speaking in some form, available to you for making new choices for full expression when you are ready. When you are out of alignment with your true purpose, you will likely experience one or more of the following conditions.

- Discontentment (with yourself / life / career / relationships / health / etc.)
- Disharmony (things don't flow easily and effortlessly)
- Disconnection (with Self and Source, as well as other people and living your life)
- Disease (a dis-ease that shows up in discomfort and physical symptoms)

Each of these states is a messenger serving as an invitation to evolve to your next best level in expressing your unique purpose.

That is the alignment process for an "illuminated" purpose... that which brings you to a new level of conscious vibration for what you want to experience in your life, including wealth. It is this harmonic alignment which helps you claim your money magic.

By being in agreement with your illuminated purpose, you are choosing to welcome new opportunities, synchronicities and resources that serve to bring you closer to Source energy AND express your unique gifts in contribution to the greater whole of community and consciousness.

Your Personal Manifestation Process

According to the dictionary, the definition of manifestation (as a noun) is as follows.

> *1 a : the act, process, or an instance of manifesting*
> *b (1) : something that manifests or is manifest*
> *(2) : a perceptible, outward, or visible expression*
> *c : one of the forms in which an individual is manifested*
> *d : an occult phenomenon; specifically : materialization*
> *2 : a public demonstration of power and purpose*

Therefore, you have created what you have in your life by some process, whether conscious or unconscious; this is your manifestation process in action. You may not have gotten exactly what you wanted with predictable or consistent results, but you did manifest what you are now experiencing.

Understand what you did to get what you currently 'got' so you can, going forward, intentionally create to get what you want in the future.

When people stop to consider how they manifest what they do, quite often the only thing they can say is that it happened under stress of some sort—a deadline, a crisis or a specific need which pressed a particular resolution into being. In reality, this is not a conscious way of manifesting your true desires. Often your true desires take a back-seat to the urgencies of life. You can, however, use the examples of your "pressure-cooker" manifesting to learn what you do so you can use it for your benefit instead of it being merely a reaction to life.

The first thing that confronts people who desire to create something new is the "not knowing" feeling which can feel destabilizing. And yet, it is exactly this feeling that creates the space to be expansive because it is the "jumping off" place for something new. The "not knowing" feeling means you need new information to orient by; it is simply a messenger illuminating to trust Source. Going further, "not knowing" can be a steppingstone to get you back into connection with Source through faith in the bigger picture you cannot see on your own.

Consider the last time you got something you really needed, even if it arrived at the last minute. Start remembering by looking at the first glimmer you had that showed it needed to happen—the awareness you needed a particular outcome. Feel how you felt when you knew you needed (or wanted) "it"—where did you feel it in your body, what were your thoughts, and what other energies were present for you in that moment (emotional responses / reactions / triggers)? Did it feel positive for you to initiate something? Were you aware of your future satisfaction? Did it just seem like things would fall into place?

These are all qualities relevant to your personal manifestation process, as well as the conditions under which you operated to create what you've already manifested. Beyond your personal process, let's explore the seven steps of manifestation.

Overview of the 7 Steps of Manifestation

Manifestation is the term which describes the result, or expression, of your power. While that statement really summarizes the concept of manifestation in entirety, there are seven specific steps you can take to support a proactive, conscious manifestation process.

Following is a summary of the seven steps of manifesting your desires; we will explore each in detail in this section.

1. Visualize Desire
2. Place Order
3. Feel Enthusiasm
4. Let Go
5. Have Trust
6. Stay in Action
7. Look for Synchronicities

Step 1: Visualize Your Desire

First, to know what will be manifest, it is vital to dream, or envision, the result of your desires. One cannot create a cake without knowing it will be a cake vs. a steak. At this point, it isn't important as to whether it is chocolate or angel food cake—the idea is to get the biggest picture of what can be for the outcome. Visualize your desire, imagining what your world will look and feel like when it has come to pass, how your life will change, who you will be when you are living the result of your desire.

It is also not important to understand how it will come to pass, nor even when it will be manifest. In fact, those thought patterns will inhibit a good visualization. When you see yourself in another country, or living an amazing lifestyle, or with the partner of your dreams, feel the entire experience. What you are doing is seeding memories in your conscious mind that help create the conditions that will allow your desires to become real.

You can use this technique to create a great meeting, a wonderful day, or a great time with a special someone. Your conscious mind is your servant that operates based on what you program into it.

By the way, that works in the opposite as well—when you focus on what you don't want, you will get what you don't want. Your conscious mind does not discern what you focus on; it processes quantity over quality, so when you focus on something, your conscious mind figures it must be important because you keep thinking about it.

Focus on what you want more of in your life—visualize your desire to initiate your manifestation process.

Step 2: Place Your Order

When you have visualized your desire (including feeling and seeing the experience of it after it has manifested), it is time to place your order with the Universe (or Source, or God, or what feels right in relating to higher consciousness).

To place your order, simply state it out loud. To give your desire even more power to manifest, write it out on a piece of paper and read it out loud twice a day. When you are reading it, recall your visualization and experience it in your body. This verbalization anchors the experience of your desire in your physical world through your body.

Remember to be as clear as possible to avoid confusion and potential miscommunication in your order; that said, your energy has more power than your words in the manifestation process. We live in a positive Universe—Source energy really does want you to have an experience in the best and highest good for you.

The bottom line: know what you want and place your order for it with clarity and feeling.

Step 3: Feel Enthusiasm

Enthusiasm is contagious and lets all your being know it's time to get ready to receive something wonderful. It is the physical expression of your desire in process of becoming manifest. Just like having enthusiasm for your guests makes them feel welcome in your home, having enthusiasm for your 'order' showing up paves the energetic way for it be embraced when it shows up.

Generating positive energy around your order becomes an attractor, like a homing beacon, for your desire to become actualized. The law of attraction says that like attracts like; when your energy vibration is high with excitement, anticipation and positive feelings, your desire matches that vibration and is drawn to you more easily. It's like a pipe which water flows through—when there is corrosion or stuck gunk, it slows down and constricts the water flow. However, when the pipe is clear and clean, more water can flow and it flows more quickly. Keep your energy high and enthusiastic around your outcome desire to help manifest it.

If you aren't sure how to feel enthusiastic for something that isn't here yet, think about when you were younger and knew your birthday was coming. Before the big day, you were excited and happy and ready to have a great birthday. That level of enthusiasm set the pace and the tone for your parents, family, and friends to contribute to your wonderful day long before the day itself. People knew you were happy and people like to be around happy people. Even more, people like to make other people happy. And so it is with the Universe delivering on your desire.

In case it's challenging to be enthusiastic about your desire, it could be your desire is not authentic. That is, a lack of enthusiasm could be a sign you need to revisit what you really want. If your desire is based on what someone else wants or is an "outgrown" desire or doesn't reflect who you are now, it is not an authentic desire.

Or it could be that there is simply too much distance between where you are and where you want to go, which shows up as blocking energy or resistance between you and that desire. In that case, identifying what exists between you and your desire gives you an action plan to take care of those blocks so you can: 1) clear the way to having your desire, and, 2) be able to have it when it shows up.

Enthusiasm is a built-in barometer that measures your ability to welcome and have your desire manifest.

Step 4: Let Go

When you know you have done what you can do to visualize your desire, place your order, feel the enthusiasm of its imminent reality, then let it go. It is time to release your attachment to the outcome and let your desire begin to grow on its own.

Gardeners do this all the time. They visualize the perfect garden and gather the ingredients to create it, whether that means tools, special soil, containers, or seeds. They get excited in working with the energy of their garden, tilling the soil, planting the seeds, feeling the beauty of what will grow. The gardener has a connection with the soil and gives thanks for being able to plant their garden, which might mean having the space, the time, or the resources to help make it happen.

Once they've planted what they can, they have to let go and trust the seeds to do their thing—to grow. If they dig up the seeds every day, the seeds don't have a chance to set roots.

Letting go has two parts... 1) releasing your attachment to the growth process, and, 2) releasing your attachment to how the outcome should occur. And it can feel destabilizing, because you are releasing what you know as familiar (even if it's dysfunctional and not working for you).

Letting go is also one of the greatest challenges people face in their lives. Look around you—what haven't you released that needs to go? Do you have clutter? Have you outgrown your relationships? What is around you that doesn't support you in who you are now? Are there any items with negative energy or bad memories associated with them? Is there room for your desire to manifest in your life?

In letting go, you open the way for the new, for your desire, to become manifest.

Remember to breathe through letting go. Why? Because when you hold your breath while you let go of something, you are still holding that energy in your physical body (which becomes stuck "gunk" over time).

Let natural intelligence take over manifesting where you leave off with your desire.

Step 5: Have Trust

Now that you have let go of your attachment to your desire, and of anything that may impede the inflow of your manifesting desire, next is to trust your desire is coming through as actualized. Trust can be elusive because it is predicated on a feeling of certainty for something that is unknown and unfamiliar as a new way of being not yet "real". However, through information you read previously in this section, you have built trust through seeing what you have already manifested. You have also clearly birthed your desire vision to the Universe. Clarity is power. If nothing else, you can trust the process to bring you what is the next right thing for you to experience.

By learning and applying a conscious manifestation process, you will get more predictable results that consistently relate to (or are predicated on) your desires.

The Universe works off what you put out energetically as well as in thought, word and action; you can see what you have manifested already based on where you were yesterday (and the day before) energetically. The good news is you can trust the Universe to deliver your current desires in manifest form—you just need to be open to follow the changes in your life that it will bring.

If you find yourself disappointed in that knowledge, consider the source of your disappointment. Is it accurate to blame the Universe for not delivering a better world for you? Or is it more accurate to say you didn't know what to ask for consciously and clearly? Did you shy away from the outcomes you didn't want, not realizing they were the fastest path to your goal if you could only confront and address them? Only you know the answer to these questions. However, when you find yourself disappointed, remember you now know how to create different results through proactively manifesting what you want.

The other nuance of having trust is allowing yourself to have your desire once it becomes manifest. Self-trust can be a key issue because we so often break promises to ourselves.

Consider the last time you were scheduled to meet with a friend who stood you up without explanation—how did you feel? What did you do the next time this friend wanted to get together? It is the same situation when considering your promises to yourself and your money. When you haven't kept promises to yourself, your self-trust is compromised and you need to earn it back through being in integrity with yourself. The most important person with whom to keep your promises is yourself.

Trust that your desire is in the process of becoming manifest; trust yourself to be able to recognize, have and enjoy it when it shows up.

Step 6: Stay in Action

Now that you have trust in yourself and the manifestation process, it's time to sit and wait, right? NOT!

Waiting is not a passive activity. Waiting is time to take care of anything that requires your energy and attention. Taking care of your to-do list could be completely unrelated to your desire. Or it could be a continuation of what you know needs to happen to foster the conditions for your desire to exist.

To return to the gardening example, the gardener trusts the seeds will grow by natural intelligence. However, the gardener's role is to water the seeds, to make sure rabbits don't eat the little seedlings, to prop the seedlings up if they fall over with a big rain or wind. Or, relative to letting go, there may be things that need to be released—excess debris around the stems, a trellis that is no longer needed. For you, maybe it's time for a spring/fall cleaning throughout your living or working space. Or maybe you need to acknowledge and honor who and what is in your life now, or what got you to where you are now. Gratitude is a powerful vibration to activate attraction energy.

You are part of a much larger whole so chances are, because you are not Tom Hanks marooned on an island with a soccer ball, there are people and current situations in your world which require your energy on some level. What do you need to do to keep energy moving? Whatever that is, do it. (Which is also the magical secret cure for procrastination, by the way.) Stay in action to keep dynamic energy in your world. You can only access the degree of energy that you use regularly (as in, you lose what you don't use).

Step 7: Look for Synchronicities

The final step of the manifestation process is to be open, aware and look for seemingly random synchronicities. There is no such thing as a coincidence, so that is your first clue as to what qualifies as a synchronicity.

A synchronicity is something out of the ordinary yet fits your desire in the bigger picture, something that is unexpected and yet right, something that triggers your awareness as being a bit out of routine occurrences. It also helps you peer into the magic of the Universe and see Source is working to deliver your desires.

For example, when you think about the next project you want to do, and the resource you need to do it just shows up, or a person you think about calls you two minutes after you thought about them, or you want to explore an area of learning and you get an email announcing a new class… these are synchronistic events.

It is important to see the signs and symbols the Universe sends to communicate important messages. The Universe may be quite literal, just like reading a billboard, or use less obvious communications, such as a commercial that repeats until you get the message. Watch for repetitive messages, unexpected invitations with social situations or opportunities, or apparently new ideas or people who show up in your world. See the connection with the bigger picture of your life and understand the power of synchronicity in delivering your desire to you in manifest form.

These are more than synchronicities—they are validation you are on your right path.

What If...?

What if what you want doesn't manifest? What if you don't recognize it, or timing is off, or the opportunities that come with it are unexpected and you somehow miss them? What if your desire manifests in an unexpected way that doesn't seem to fit your order?

Playing the "what if" game keeps you out of being present right here and now. It is based on future potentials that may or may not occur and is a sign your trust in the manifestation process is not comprehensive.

That said, when you are in trust and integrity with the seven steps to manifesting your desires, you may find opportunities present as "steppingstones" to the final manifestation of your desire. That is, things, circumstances, people, and situations present where you have active choice in what occurs next and may not be what you thought would come up or look like when you originally placed your order. The message is you must be in perception of what occurs throughout your manifestation process because the Universe might have something much greater in mind if you are open to accept it.

Some of these steps may change their order or ask you to revisit them throughout the manifestation process. When that occurs, it's generally a sign you haven't completed that step, or the Universe needs a little more energy in that place, or additional clarification will help manifest your desire more thoroughly.

Do not take it personally or allow your ego to hold you back from completing that step. Just because there is more information needed or you need to do something else does not mean something is wrong with the process. Simply know it will pay off in the enhanced manifestation of your desire when it arrives. Flow through that step by following and supporting the energy required for you to show up in the best way to support the manifestation of what you want.

The Universe will deliver the best and highest version of your order based on what you have asked for, what's happening for you in the moment and what's possible for you in the biggest picture. To recognize your successful manifestation process when working with positive energy, here's the bottom line...

When it's light, it feels right.

Claiming Your Money Magic

There are big things happening in the world, and people cannot play big—BE big—when they're worrying about money. Worse, if they're putting their best creative energies into figuring out how to fit into a box that was never designed for them, just enough to pay their bills, then the world isn't receiving the benefit of their natural gifts and talents. This is the when we need everybody showing up in full force to help us get to our collective next best level. You actively claiming your money magic is essential to creating an abundant future for all of us.

This section covered a lot of material about how to find your formula in claiming your money magic, beginning with the Money Magic Formula.

$$\frac{\text{Perception x Your Choices x Action Taken}}{\text{Resistance to Change}} = \text{Outcome (Money)}$$

This discovery journey explored how your expanded perception plus your conscious choice and the actions you took (both physically and energetically) are divided by your resistance to change. If your resistance to change is significant, your perception, choices, and actions will have a limited effect on your outcome (your money).

Then we covered the Three Keys to Wealth: Self-Nurturing, Illumination of Purpose, and Personal Manifestation Process. This included such concepts as you are your own currency, it's vital you live from your illuminated and aligned purpose, and your personal manifestation process will follow a seven-step process you can use to intentionally create what you want.

Be aware of your money magic and the power you have in every moment to claim it so you can be the conscious creator you are with your wealth (and everything in your experience).

The Rituals
of Creating Money:
Ways to Play to Get More
of What You Want

Discover Rituals for Your Money

This chapter is designed to help you understand how to use personal rituals to harness the power of various levels of energy to support attracting, creating, and having more money.

We will consider how rituals relate to the process of money manifestation, as well as what to watch for in your experience with rituals and give guidance on specific, proven rituals you can do in practical ways. Part of the power of ritual comes from tapping into the energies of what other people have done to leverage that same or similar energy for your own results.

Please know these are ways that can open you to receiving and shifting your energy, but they aren't "truths". That is, they will only work if you are open to and use them. There is no harm done if you aren't open to using rituals; however, remember this is all about shifting your energy by working with energy on some level. Think of rituals as "tools" that, when you feel they are the best tool to get the result(s) you want, you can use them that way. The tools you like and are comfortable with are the ones you will be drawn to use; conversely, the ones you have no resonance with are the ones you will likely ignore without any negative side effects.

A note for expectations management: teaching you how to simply do a ritual and then expect big changes immediately is not the point of this book. This is all about supporting you in working with Source energy proactively and deliberately for your personal creation process. It's intended to be an introduction to a real-world, sustainable way to work with energy that permeates all of your life and physically anchors your energetic manifestation process.

These rituals have been passed down, in some cases, for generations; they come from various esoteric practices, including Feng Shui, energy tapping, power affirmations, moon magic and others. You will also see linear methods to approach ritual from the rational mind as both sides of your brain offer valuable resources to any creation process. Use all the tools, resources and energy available to you to help you create more of what you want—including money. (BONUS: with some minor modification, you can likely use a form of these rituals to create in other areas of your life too!)

Here's to the rituals that can support and empower you in creating money.

The Definition and Importance of Rituals

"Real wealth is ideas plus energy."
~ Richard Buckminster Fuller, Architect

A ritual is simply time, space and/or process reserved for and dedicated to something sacred that you personally hold as important or significant. There is a lot of "mystery", or connection to the mystical realms, associated with rituals. While that is partially attributable to the highest form of honor for rituals as a sacred tool, it is a bit misleading in that the common person often believes they themselves can't perform or aren't somehow worthy or specially trained enough to perform rituals. That is simply not true.

Rituals have the power of working directly with universal energies to set intentions, release energy for positive transformation and clear space in the physical and metaphysical realms. On a daily basis, you have bathing and dressing rituals, although you likely don't consider them as the powerful rituals they are… so consider how your day is different when you are unable to complete these personal daily preparation rituals.

So a ritual does not have to be complicated to be effective, although there are some rituals which have a lot of moving parts to them. The power generator of a ritual is in the energy you hold toward it. Your emotional connection is what makes the ritual come into being in the first place and, without your energy, there is no reason for the ritual. The ritual is a way for you to honor what you value most, set intention in motion and create the space for a manifestation experience to occur on some level (physical, energetic, emotional, financial, spiritual, etc.).

It should be noted some people have not taken advantage of ritual due to fear, religious beliefs, or extreme discomfort; however, ritual is about you creating sacred space for what is important to you. It is NOT about religion or even about a moral right/wrong perspective. It is not about replacing your spiritual beliefs on any level; if anything, it is to enhance what you believe and desire for yourself by adding focused energy and intention to what is important to you. Rituals have nothing to do with your religious orientation; however, you must be comfortable in deciding how you feel best in communicating and focusing your energy so pay attention to what feels good for you.

If rituals "read", or feel, like a positive method for you to direct and honor your energy, read on…

Three Levels of Working with Energy

"It is only when you have both divine grace and human endeavor that you can experience bliss, just as you can enjoy the breeze of a fan only when you have both a fan and the electrical energy to operate it."

~ Sri Sathya Sai Baba, Guru

There are levels of energy and, therefore, levels of ritual you can use to activate action toward what you want and desire. Since I am not a scientist, I won't go into the specifics of all the different kinds of energy from that definition. Instead, it's more important you experience different levels of energy in your mind's eye for just a moment based on what you've already experienced in your life—that will give you the best definition of energy because it is based on what you know and have a frame of reference for it.

Consider an environment of someone you know and care about—pick the messiest one. Maybe they have papers on the floor, boxes of stuff to be unpacked, unfinished decorating projects or clothes and papers all over the place. Imagine yourself in that environment and, as much as you care for your loved one, consider what it would take to make that environment feel good. It's likely you would start simply by picking up the mess.

That is an example of a mundane energy issue and the solution being mundane; it becomes a ritual based on how you approach it. If you hold the space in a sacred way, taking care to 'heal' the environment with time and personal attention (even if you're moving fast) vs. resenting the pick-up of things and passing judgment and projecting your disapproval on your loved one for letting it get to that state, you can imagine the qualitative difference in energy.

Let's go a step further...

Once that same environment is cleaned up, sorted out and the mundane basics are handled, now you see some of the furniture doesn't quite feel right. Maybe it doesn't fit, or the styles of various pieces clash, or they are worn and need replacing. You would need to adjust these items accordingly. So you would likely repair, remove, or replace whatever isn't working in that environment so it would 'flow' and be at its most attractive state. That is an example of 'adjusting' the space, which is the second level of ritual. It is handling the refinements needed to optimize the situation in a tangible way.

Lastly, once you have handled the mundane level of working with the environment, and then adjusted the items in it for optimal presentation and functionality, you would need to 'feel' the energy of the space. Imagine you walked into that same room after two people had an argument in it—what would that feel like? What if you walked into it after there was a celebration party—how would that feel? The difference you would experience in your sensations in that space is the 'transcendental' quality of energy as it has been activated in that environment. This is the third, and most powerful, level of ritual as it is connecting with the Source energy present in that space; however, to make the most of it, you really need to work with the first two levels. Meaning, working with transcendental energy does not have the same power when things are a mess.

You have just experienced the three levels of energy and ritual we will be working with in this book: 1) mundane, 2) adjustment, and, 3) transcendental. Throughout this chapter, there are realistic tools that work directly with universal energies, which is not something most people are likely to consider on a consistent basis.

Three Levels of Symbolism

"Life is a symbol to be lived."
~ John Fire Lame Deer, Medicine Man

An important aspect of ritual is the use of symbolism. Why? Because, for example, it's hard to reference you want the strength of a bear and use an actual bear in your intention ceremony.

Symbols have three levels of relevance to any one person. The level which is "furthest" from you is universal symbology; that is, universal symbols of wealth relate to all people anywhere. An example of a universal symbol of wealth is your stove, because in any culture anywhere in the world, when you have the ability to use the stove to cook nourishment, it indicates you have the means to buy/get food. Make sure your stove is in good working order, that all the burners work, and rotate using all the burners regularly. Sometimes people tend to cook on just one burner out of four, which limits their ability to generate wealth energy to just 25% of their potential.

The second layer of symbolic representation is cultural, which is something that has meaning for the country or culture in which you live. For people in the United States, the Liberty Bell would have special meaning, but people from other countries may not know or care about it.

And the third layer, which is most important because it is the clos-est to you, is comprised of the personal symbols which have meaning for you. Such objects might be the first dollar you ever earned, your childhood piggy bank, or a copy of your first paycheck. These objects hold meaning for you, but others would not relate to them the same way you do. These symbols are actually the most powerful in acti-vating your environment because you have an emotional connection to them.

By using symbols, you are referencing something greater than the item itself. This is a powerful way to invite the infinite intensity of the consciousness of that item into your world.

Reinforcement of the Three Secrets

> *"All the breaks you need in life wait within your imagination. Imagination is the workshop of your mind, capable of turning mind energy into accomplishment and wealth."*
>
> ~ Napoleon Hill, Author

To fully activate a ritual, it is important to use the Reinforcement of the Three Secrets. Essentially, this means to think it, say it, and do it at the same time.

For example, when you place a ritual object in a certain area, think about what and why you are doing it, then say out loud your desired outcome, and place the object (to complete the ritual) at the same time. One example of the statement you make might be "I am placing this _____ here to honor abundance coming to me in all ways in my best and highest good. And so it is....".

The Reinforcement of the Three Secrets is said to increase the power of your ritual in a significant way. This makes logical sense, because you are engaging more of your senses in the energetic component of your manifestation process. More importantly, it invokes more energy on more levels to support you in having what you want.

How Rituals Relate to Creating Money

"And what is a man without energy?
Nothing—nothing at all."
~ Mark Twain, Author

With focus, the power of energy changes in its ability to affect a given area. Consider the common light bulb—it is diffused light capable of illuminating a dark space or room. Now consider the laser beam, which is made of concentrated, focused light particles, capable of slicing through some of the densest materials known to mankind. Both are light—the only difference being one is more intensely focused than the other. That is the power of your focused intention in terms of your own manifestation process.

A ritual is only possible when you know what you want to achieve and take action that is focused on calling in the intangible resources to actualize it in the physical world. It is through your focus you communicate your desires to the Universe. And a ritual is the modality by which you communicate your desires.

So when you have the desire to create something in your life, which, in this case, is more money, you can call it in faster by using the power of focus in a ritual. There are some suggested rituals you can use, but, as with anything in life, feel free to personalize and/or create your own for as well.

How to Measure Outcomes of Rituals

"The more you lose yourself in something bigger
than yourself, the more energy you will have."
~ Norman Vincent Peale, Minister

Once you've completed a ritual, it is important to watch for signs and synchronicities. The Universe speaks through symbolic language, which means you will get messages through such things as pictures, images, circumstances, connections, and opportunities. To both see and understand them, it's best to be detached from what you think they should look like when they arrive. By releasing your expectation as to how they should show up or what they should look like or even what they say, you will be open to what comes. And that is a powerful place to be when working with Source energy.

When you are not attached to the outcome of how your ritual shows up in exact form, you allow 'wiggle room' for the Universe to bring you your request—and sometimes even better!

For example, one client asked for greater abundance and found she got checks in the mail from people sending unexpected gifts, her car was serviced for free, her computer was fixed for the cost of parts only (not the hundreds it could have been for professional time fees), her property manager paid an apartment fee and her landlord paid for gardening fees—none of which was expected and all of which shifted her enjoyment of abundance. She received far more than she asked for, because she was open to anything that came to her.

You may also be guided to take actions in a new way, which will yield new results, such as following through on connecting with friends of friends, someone you met at a coffee shop or a local contact you discovered through Facebook or another social networking site. Each of these new actions will generate new energy and may result in additional revenues in some way.

The key is to increase your awareness and perception of what is happening in your world in the moment because there are no accidents or coincidences; you asked for these things to come into your life on some level. Remember, this is how you empower yourself to create. When you don't 'own' the results you've already achieved in your life (regardless of your level of happiness with them), a ritual will be hard-pressed to create beyond what you are feel you are responsible for and capable of creating in your life.

Recall the three levels of working with energy, beginning with the mundane. If you have not claimed the power on the most mundane level (in this case, your ability to create all that is in your life up until now), the transcendental energy will bring you limited results because you are disempowering your connection to Source energy. When you are clear you are where you are as a result of your choices, decisions and actions, and that your results are yours alone (whatever they may be), you give yourself the power to manifest much more powerfully.

So look for validation your rituals are working by paying attention to the signs, which can show up any time, any place, in any form. It might be in a billboard, in overhearing a casual conversation, or the sign on a bus or truck... it's up to you to be aware of the signs. As you do so, you will develop your understanding of the personal language of your rituals.

Money, Abundance and Prosperity Rituals

"Nothing can add more power to your life than
concentrating all your energies on a limited set of targets."
~ Nido Qubein, President of High Point University

There are rituals you can use to work with universal energies to attract wealth and abundance in the forms of money, opportunities, and prosperity. Following are suggested rituals you can use; however, I recommend you use only one at a time so you can work with the incoming energies more easily.

Believe it or not, carrying a $100 bill with you at all times is a ritual. It is insurance that you always have money and is a "seed" for attracting and growing more money. By always feeling abundant, you are connecting with Source energy consistently—and that strengthens your ability to enjoy more wealth in your life.

A simple guideline would be to initiate a ritual every 27 days, ideally coinciding with the new moon. The new moon supports bringing new ideas to life, so it is an ideal time to set your intentions.

One of my personal favorites is a ritual called a "mock-up", where you literally make a mock-up of your intentions coming to reality and releasing that desire energy to Source for handling. To do this ritual, take a clean piece of paper. Draw a "balloon" shape with the tail at the bottom of the page—make the balloon any size you want. Then write inside the balloon what you want in as much detail as you can… include everything from the tangible results to letting go of what's not needed—this is the time to put it all in there, because it's ideal to capture as much information as possible when you are setting your intention.

Once you've completed the full documentation of your mock-up, add this phrase within your balloon: "… in my best and highest good." This phrase lets the Universe know you trust the bigger picture.

Then add a 'tail' to the bottom of your balloon (like a string), then draw a horizontal line across the bottom where the string attaches (think where the earth is and up springs a plant, similar to a child quickly drawing grass). On the string (or stem of your balloon), add a "leaf" shape—this is "wiggle room" for the Universe to bring you a more expansive interpretation of your request (as well as opening your mock-up to the discretion of the Universe, which can give you not only what you ask for but possibly something better).

Then take this piece of paper outside and burn it in a safe place. The most potent times of day to complete this part of the ritual are between 11:00 and 1:00, either am or pm.

Remember to use the Harmony of Three Secrets—to think it, say it, do it ("I am burning this to set intentions and release the energy around having more money…"). As the smoke is releasing, know your intentions are being carried safely to Source energy for activation. Make sure the fire is out and there are only ashes left.

The Universe knows the "right" way for you to receive and delivers exactly what you want and need. The reality is that, typically, we humans get in the way and prevent our own flow. Rituals are the tool that helps connect with your greatness through your intentions and supports it (including wealth) to become a reality.

The Importance of Keeping It Sacred

It is also helpful to keep your rituals private by not sharing with others. Sharing dilutes the power of your ritual by breaching the sacredness of the ritual for yourself (think balloon with little pinholes in it caused by each share). In some cases, it may be appropriate to ask for synergy from others to see your intentions become manifest; however, that is a situation that requires discernment. When you do choose to share, take care about who you share it with and ask for their combined focus to empower your intention through your ritual to bring you your desired results.

Once you've completed your ritual, you must know it is working for you like you know you are breathing—without question. Where there is doubt, there is potentially an obstacle; if this is the case, understand what is in the way, address it according to what you know and begin the ritual again (or create another).

You may want to clear your house of any excess or non-supporting energies; there are several ways to do this. You can burn sage and allow the smoke to take the energy away (you would light a sage stick, blow out the flames so it smokes, and walk through your space one room at a time with the fumes wafting through your space). You can clap in each room, especially in dark corners, to move the energy in your space. You can use citrus aromatherapy to release unhealthy energy. And there are other ways to do space clearings as well. The point is to connect with the energy of your space and help it get rid of whatever no longer belongs there.

Begin with the End in Mind

It is also important to be in gratitude and feel good about receiving, including what you have already received and what you trust is on the way in the largest picture. You can ask for what you want over and over again, but that really won't accomplish what you seek. You are not limited, the asking is not limited… it's your ability to receive that is limited. By being in gratitude, you are acknowledging your ability to receive.

Remember you are "co-creating" your life experience with universal energies and you have already experienced manifesting where you are now. If you were not meant to be where you are for whatever reason, even if it is learning some painful lessons, you would not be there.

By the by, "co-creating" is a bit of a misnomer, just as your hands are "co-hands", operating distinctly from you. It's not really true you are "co-creating" with Source because you ARE the creator in physical form. But that's a digression for now...

By reading this book, you are indicating you are ready to move on. So here are several different rituals you can use to achieve your goals.

Open the Door to Receiving

This is a transcendental ritual, meaning you are working directly with the energy. When you want to make and hold on to your money, get a clear jar with a lid and place coins and bills in it. Once you have secured the lid, place it in the Wealth area of your home (basically, stand at your front door, then look all the way to the left-side back corner of your home). It is not necessary for this jar to be visible for it to work on your behalf because you are in direct connection with universal energies. Once placed, leave the jar untouched for at least 27 days. If you move it, simply begin the ritual again.

Your front door is where the Universe brings you prosperity, opportunities, and wealth. Make sure your front door is inviting, and that your doorbell, front door light and front door are all in good working order. Make sure your front door can open all the way (as in, nothing is behind it or blocking it from being able to open completely). Your street number should be easily visible from the street at night. And you want to use your front door at least once a week (if not daily) so energy flows openly through it, bringing wealth along with it.

When you want more money to come to your front door, get nine I-Ching coins (Chinese money with square holes in the center) and thread a nine-inch piece of red ribbon through their centers (make sure all the coins are facing the same way). Tie the two ends of the ribbon together. Place the coins under your front door mat with the more active side of the coins up (that's the side with the most symbols on it). Be sure to use the Reinforcement of the Three Secrets for maximum activation. (One of my clients actually received two unexpected checks and a job offer within 48 hours of doing this ritual.)

When you want your money to grow, take nine new bills of any denomination and place them in a red envelope. Red envelopes have been used for generations to signify the complete cycle of the transformation of energy; for example, Feng Shui practitioners get paid in red envelopes because the services have been performed for the client and the client pays for the services. (You can get red envelopes at Feng Shui supply stores or even on Amazon.) You can use that same principle in requesting a result from the Universe; make your request in a red envelope, and the return will be the granting of your request to complete the energetic cycle.

To continue this particular ritual, take the nine new bills, seal them into the red envelope, and place them in your Wealth area to grow. Leave the envelope until you have attained the results you want. One client grew her clientele—and revenues!—by 30% when using this ritual within just three weeks.

When you want to attract abundance in different ways, use a treasure box. Find a box that represents the container into which good things will come—it can be as simple or as ornate as you feel is right. Write out the characteristics, qualities, or items you would like to manifest, and place them in the box. Be careful to not ask for things that conflict with each other, because they may cancel each other out, such as a more active social life and more alone time to rejuvenate. Place this box in your Wealth area for at least 27 consecutive days, then watch for synchronicities and signs that your request(s) is being fulfilled.

Observe Both Sides

In fact, you can use where you are asking the Universe for opposites as an opportunity to understand what is blocking your request or asking for your attention. This situation could be a valuable clue as to why you have been getting different results than what you expected in your previous requests. As you consider where you are asking for outcomes that conflict with each other, you can clarify your intention, re-interpret your previous results for alignment with your ability to manifest in a bigger way than you thought or set more than one intention in motion now.

You can also place objects in your treasure box, such as spices, feathers, crystals, or anything else that holds the vibration of what you want to attract. You can even write a check to yourself for the money you want (rumor has it that this was part of Jim Carrey's success in becoming a known actor). If it feels right to you, you can place the treasure box under your bed so you work with these energies while sleeping; however, take caution in doing so, as this may disrupt your sleeping patterns.

As stated at the beginning of this book, follow what is right for you—your own wisdom supersedes anything in this book. In fact, remember to modify these rituals as feels comfortable for you as well— these are simply reference guides for what could work for you. If you don't have a particular suggested item, feel free to substitute or even eliminate that item. (In fact, sometimes part of the ritual includes what you need to do to assemble your ritual items… the energy begins building as the physical pieces of your ritual come together.)

Use the Reinforcement of the Three Secrets while placing the treasure box in your Wealth or Helpful People area, according to the Feng Shui Bagua map. To find these areas in your home, imagine you are flying over your house and you can see a visual "tic-tac-toe" grid over your house, with the bottom of the grid being the wall that contains your front door. The Wealth area will be the furthest left-diagonal third (at the back of the house from the front door) and the Helpful People area will be the closest right-hand third of your space (immediately to the right of the front door; in fact, your front door may enter into the Helpful People area). In either case, by placing your treasure box in these areas, you are "activating" the energy of that particular area consciously to bring you whatever intentions you have energized in your treasure box.

Other activators for Wealth include water fountains (flowing water is flowing money), the number 8 (meaning eight items or the number 8), the colors green / purple / red. You can also decorate using pictures of Wealth in this area quite effectively. And this is an ideal place to position a vision board, or collage of what you intend to do / be / have in your life. A quick note: if you choose to have a water fountain in this area, make sure you can see where the water comes out and where the water is stored; if any part of the water stream is hidden, it can result in draining your money away.

Create a Manifestation Board

A personal ritual you may want to create is a "manifestation board". On a piece of paper, or on a whiteboard, draw a vertical line down the middle. On the left side (which is the receiving side), write out all your existing financial needs (rent/mortgage, car payment, etc.) and, on the right, write out all your wants—everything you want to have in your life you don't have currently. This list can include anything from a massage to a vacation… it is important to list what you want to enjoy as a gift to yourself as a counterbalance to the necessary expenses on the left side. The manifestation board acts as a way to communicate to the Universe exactly what you need and want, thereby allowing it to manifest more cleanly. Personally, I also use this to track not only my expenses but credit card balances as well so the Universe can help me pay those off. (This was so successful that I paid down my credit card debt by six figures in just 14 months.)

You can also use your dreams to create wealth. Thirty minutes before you actually go to sleep (not thirty minutes before you climb into bed), focus on any questions or situations involving money and ask that you receive your answers during your sleep time. When you wake up in the morning, be sure to note the first things you remember from your dreams. Later, when you're more awake, review those notes to distill and interpret your wealth messages.

While awake, you can use your mental projector, or intellectual white screen, to get messages. In your mind's eye, imagine a large white screen (like a projector screen) in front of you. Make sure there is nothing on it. Then focus on your question or issue and ask your messages to appear on the white board. Note: you may see images, words or even vignettes; write down what you see. When complete with the visioning, take time to review your notes so you can understand your money messages.

Similarly, you can ask a trusted friend to be your screen for your money movie. Play out your money movie verbally to your friend, and have your friend repeat it back to you. See how it feels to watch your own movie; if you need to make changes, simply "re-wind" and play it again (just like you would a DVD). Keep doing this until your movie is exactly the way you want it; this process makes real your emotional connection to your money movie which activates the manifestation energy toward what you want.

Another quick note: pay attention to who you are associating with as a reflection of your money vibration. When everyone you know is struggling for money, chances are you are too. Increase your money vibration by hanging out with people who have, and are comfortable with having, money. This can be a great way to learn about how to shift your personal relationship with money—by observing and being present to how others positively relate to their money.

You may also want to declare your money intentions and goals out loud twice daily. The vibration of your voice, along with your breath as you in-spire (breathe in) is the vibration of your essence, which is the key to manifestation on the physical plane. It's all about energy so stating your money intentions verbally in the morning and evening helps align your energy with your incoming wealth. While doing so, stand with your feet shoulder-width apart and "swivel" or sway your hips in a figure 8 (at least three times); this clears physical energy that may be stuck around your money energy. Bonus: taking walks, using an elliptical, running on a treadmill all move your hips so they all support movement in your money energy.

Expand Your Capacity

There are other "stretching" rituals you can do to increase your money capacity in the physical world. You can go house or car shopping, visit places of abundance, or plan your dream vacation. Again, this is about going beyond where you've been and allowing your unconscious mind to create so your linear mind gets to figure out how to keep up with what you are generating on an energetic level.

You may want to try the Emotional Freedom Technique (EFT) as a way to release the stuck energy around money that is in your physical and etheric bodies. This is a "tapping" technique that focuses on the energy meridians in your body, combined with verbal guidance you recite as you tap, which can be a powerful way to shift your vibration around money. (Note: there are other, better resources than this book which can help explain exactly how to use this particular technique.)

Consider having a "big money ideas" book for yourself; this is where you note all your thoughts about big money—everything from attracting it to creating it to making it to enjoying it. By having all the energy of your big money thoughts in one place, you have focused, concentrated energy that allows a clear connection with the Universe (and yourself) about your emerging / new relationship with money.

It is important to release what is not yours or is non-supporting around your money. It's also important to understand your own manifestation language, messages, and process. Every aspect of your relationship with money must be clear of stuck, stagnant, unsupportive, or inherited beliefs and behaviors.

Of course, you can also create your own rituals for wealth. The important elements of ritual are that the ritual resonates with you, the items you use have meaning for you, the intention is positive and doesn't cause intentional harm, and that you are clearly thinking, saying and doing your intention statement and ritual action. This is your personal manifestation process, so it needs to reflect YOU in every way for optimal power. [1]

Money Exercises

"Trusting your intuition means tuning in as deeply as you can to the energy you feel, following that energy moment to moment, trusting that it will lead you where you want to go and bring you everything you desire."
~ Shakti Gawain, Author

Exercise helps you practice your discoveries. In the case of shifting your relationship with Wealth, there is a lot of internal work that can be done to change your abundance patterns. Consider the following exercises—when one or more resonate with you, take time to follow through on doing the exercise for yourself.

100 Do / Be / Have Exercise

Write out 100 things you will do, have and/or be with or as a result of the abundance, wealth, money that you want to enjoy. The idea is that everything is one place, from having weekly facials to owning a second home in Hawaii. It's harder than it looks so give yourself some time to work through this exercise. Bonus: follow through on those you can do right now with where you are; for example, if one of them is to have time to read more books, start making time to read more books each week. This will support your money energy because, for you, reading books means you are abundant.

Examine Your Belief Systems Exercise

Write the word "money" at the top of a clean sheet of paper. Now write down, in free association, anything that comes to your mind about that word—write down everything as fast as you can. This includes beliefs, thoughts, ideas, associations… everything. Now do the same with the following words: cash, debt, income, earning, giving money, receiving money, rich people, revenue.

When done with these lists, review them for the "greater truths" in them. For example, you might see you think money is only for celebrities or beautiful people or you aren't worthy of receiving (only giving) or you don't want to make more money than your parents did or money has to be earned (vs. gifted, won, inherited, etc.).

Once you've discovered your core beliefs about money, dissolve them by making a positive intention statement. Such a statement might be something like "From this point forward, I know I am worthy of receiving financial abundance from all sources in my best and highest good."

Note the last part—"in my best and highest good—is "insurance" to allow wiggle room to make abundance flow in the best way for you. A Feng Shui ritual would be to burn these lists once you're finished with them, offering the energy in them to be released to the Universe for transformation so you no longer carry their energy as it no longer serves you to keep it. Bury the ashes under a new plant to signify new growth.

What Are Your Excuses? Exercise

When you think about money, why you don't have money, or what to say when you can't go out with friends or pay a bill, what are your excuses? Do you say something about how you need a raise, or say you are taking action to generate more money or say you are changing your spending choices? The idea is to find your personal "little white lies" to yourself so you can honestly confront them through conscious awareness.

Your Five Closest Friends Exercise

Consider your five closest friends, determine what you think is their annual income, then divide that number by five. Chances are you will be within ten percent of that number either way. If you want to increase your money, hang out with people who make more money.

Invite a Friend Exercise

Ask a friend or an acquaintance to come and view your home/office environment as a stranger. It's helpful to invite someone who you respect to visit for this exercise (and it's a bonus if you feel comfortable in their space as well). The goal of this inspection is to let you see your space through someone else's eyes. What do they observe about your money as a result of being in your space? This is about being honest, taking in a different view, and determining if there is merit in taking action on things you were unable to see on your own.

Financial Contract Exercise

Draw up a financial contract with yourself. Make sure it has specific, measurable goals. Include timeframes, possible venues to generate money, and sign it just like any other contract. This document then contains the power of your intentions, so you must treat it like you would any contractual obligation to make things happen.

Learn About Money Exercises

To educate yourself on how money works, who has money and how they have it, surround yourself with (and use) resources to learn about money. Whether through audio or videotapes, books, webinars, telesummits, teleclasses, personal coaching, or conferences, get really comfortable with the subject of money. It is an unspoken taboo to talk about personal income; however, you can find many resources about money in general.

Attraction Plan Exercise

Write down a list of what you want to attract into your life—not necessarily the how, but the what. If it's a particular type of job or kind of client, write out all the specifics of what that looks like. Then write a list of all you are willing to do so you can be attractive to that energy, such as being healthy (which means working out, eating right, sleeping well....). Remember like energy attracts like energy, and it is literal—you must be prepared to be in integrity between what you want to attract and what you are capable of attracting. Once you have these lists, place them in your Wealth area. Make sure to follow through on the mundane aspects of showing up as you need to so you can maximize your attraction factor with the desired energy.

Double Your Income Plan Exercise

Determine how much money you want to bring in each month. Then create a plan to bring in double that amount each month. For example, if you want $5,000 a month, create a plan that will bring in $10,000 a month. What would you do right now if you were dropped into your own environment with the skills you have and needed to generate $10,000 in the next 30 days? Get creative—use all your resources.

This is zero-based thinking, starting from the beginning. It is amazing what can happen when you start to get outside the self-imposed limits you are working in now. How badly do you want more money? Your plan can show you how to generate income in ways you may have never considered before.

Five Minutes a Day Exercise

Identify the steps you want to take to make change in your wealth, whether it is cleaning a closet, hanging a picture or a ritual. Then break that into five-minute increments and do them. Over the course of a week, five minutes a day is 35 minutes and, over the course of a month, five minutes daily becomes more than two hours! Anything can be achieved with time and attention, even if it is bite-sized pieces.

Giving Exercise

When is the last time you gave freely and unconditionally from the heart? We know whatever we give comes back ten-fold. If you have withheld your time, attention, money or love, chances are you have not been receiving much of the same. Giving is a tool for receiving, so you can activate your receiving by giving of yourself in some way (although remember, nothing is actually required for you to do in order to receive—this just opens up the energy in a bigger way for you).

Money Mantra Exercise

Whenever fears around money come up, have a money mantra ready to address them, such as "I easily and effortlessly pay all my bills and living expenses". Reinforcing you have and are receiving what you need and want is the best way to dissolve the fears around scarcity.

Money Mindset Exercises

Inspiring yourself by having a money mindset means working with your self-talk, core belief systems and higher self. Create and use "I Am" statements, such as "I am successful by _____" or "I know I am successful by_____" or "I am enjoying abundance through _____". Meditate to clear your mind and path. Visualize for eleven minutes a day where you want to be financially so you focus on what you want and "feel" already living it—see it as your own movie in how you are living your abundant money—today.

It can be supportive to use affirmation statements in the morning and in the evening before sleep to re-program your thinking. Create your intention statements to power your daily actions and work with universal energies to help you achieve your financial goals. The idea is to reprogram your money mindset and allow your feelings to energize your money mindset.

Change It Up Exercise

When something changes, everything around it changes in response—it's simple cause and effect, which is universal law. Basically, a triggering event, or cause, will create an outcome, or effect. When you want to create new outcomes, you have to change something—essentially, create a new "cause" that generates a new "effect".

So, move your stuff around, change the "footprint" of your space, and there will be a new effect. When you change the placement of one thing in your space daily for 27 days in a row, at the end of 27 days, you are creating change.

You can also change your habits, your schedule, your food intake… it is only by doing something new that you can get new results.

Life Inventory Exercises

No matter what exercise you choose, you are taking action by using any one of them to reveal and activate your internal belief systems about money, wealth, and prosperity.

> *"A rock pile ceases to be a rock pile the moment a single man contemplates it, bearing within him the image of a cathedral."*
>
> ~ Antoine de Saint-Exupéry, Author

This is an overall look at how abundance, wealth and money show up in your life on a daily basis. Completing this exercise is a reality check, and vividly demonstrates where it may be possible to reallocate your resources.

In this section, you'll surface aspects of abundance that are important to you. Please have a piece of paper and something to write with handy to take notes and complete the following exercises.

Qualities

A. Describe the qualities you feel are the most abundant about you and your lifestyle now.

(Examples: openness to new ideas, able to sleep in or not use an alarm clock, have a latte daily, etc.)

B. Describe or list the qualities that might disappear if you become abundant.

(Examples: integrity, honesty, friendliness, and ability to relate to people, etc.)

Activities

List activities you enjoy now and want to continue to enjoy when you are abundant.

(Examples: family dinners, annual vacation weekend, time to watch TV, etc.)

Beliefs

A. Describe beliefs you have about money.

(Examples: it doesn't grow on trees, have to work hard to get it, rich people do certain things or act differently, etc.)

B. Describe beliefs about money that you *want* to have now

(Examples: I am worthy of being wealthy, money comes to me easily, etc.)

Other Things

What are some other things about your life you refuse to give up, just to be rich?

These are some of the ways you currently relate to money. By identifying, examining, and naming them, you are choosing to continue to keep that relationship with money.

Now to consider what money could mean to your lifestyle. What changes do you anticipate? In what ways will being rich allow your soul to flourish? What will you have, do, and feel when you are rich that you can't now? Where will you live? What qualities, experiences, enrichment, will you afford that you can't now?

Things You Want to Have

Let's start with some things you want to have. Make a written list with two columns. List an item on the left and its' potential effect on your happiness in the right column. There may be things that will not necessarily have a soul connection—it's ok to simply list a plasma screen TV. Make your list as comprehensive as possible.

Things You Want to Do

What about experiences and things you want to do? These could be one-time events, like travel to a place you've not been able to afford to go, like have dinner at an exquisite restaurant, or they could be on-going experiences like moving to a new location, getting education, taking up a hobby, or funding a cause.

List things you will do in first week or month after you become rich.

Qualities

What qualities about your life will be enhanced or brought into existence either directly by being wealthy or by being able to have or do some of the things you've described? Examples include status and prestige, finally enjoying a hobby, time to mentor young people, proving to others that you've "made it". Reserve self-judgment on whether these qualities seem out of place or character as the priority is to express them.

Time

How will you spend your time differently when you are rich? Sleep late? Get up early? Take more vacations? What will you do for work? (Even Bill Gates has to do something when he gets up in the morning.) Who will you spend your valuable time with?

A. What will you start doing, or do more of, when you're rich?

B. What will you stop doing, or do less of, when you're rich?

The insights of this section were designed to discover why you want to enjoy money. It is important to understand your own motivations so you can work with what pulls you forward. At this point, you are becoming more aware of changes you could make in your internal environment to create a greater relationship with wealth in your life.

Environment

A. Write a paragraph describing your current living environment with include as much clarity as possible. My home is: _____.

B. Write a paragraph about your future living environment when you have reached the point of being abundant. Include as much description as possible. My home is:

_____.

C. In exercise A immediately above, replace the words of "my home" and "my house" with the words "my life". What does that say to you now?

D. List your top ten values.

For example: creativity, honesty, clarity, love, truth, innovation, freedom, spirituality, family, etc.

Now consider where these values are reflected in your home, or if they are even present at all. When they are not reflected in your environment, there is a "disconnect" between you and living abundantly according to your inner compass.

E. Look around you as you are sitting right now. Is there anything that "pings", "stings" or has a "charge" in your mind when you see it? Is there anything broken or dirty? Are there places of clutter or piles of things that you've been meaning to get handled? Are you tolerating a squeaky door or unfinished projects? If you answered yes to any of the above, make a to-do list, then start working it as quickly as possible.

Altogether, you now have a new priority action plan to start living more abundantly. Remember your environment is your mirror; if your mirror shows a poverty mindset, it will continue to be reinforced and could add to your money inertia.

My Intention For You

"A billion here and a billion there, and pretty soon you're
talking real money."
~ Everett Dirksen, Politician

Remember wealth is everything—your thoughts, where you spend your time, the environment that surrounds you in every way. Be conscious of where you are putting your energy, whether it is time management, relationships or old "programs" running in your head.

By completing this inventory of your life, you may have discovered things you want to keep—and things you recognize need to change so you can be more abundant.

As a disclaimer, I obviously cannot guarantee your success in creating money. However, by reading this and seeing your relationship with money in a new way should, ideally, change things up for your cash flow. My intention is you can now more easily create the money you want and need on demand. When you do, I'd love to celebrate that with you so be sure to drop me a line to let me know how you are doing.

How to Make Friends with Your Money as an Entrepreneur

Your Relationship with Money Affects Everything

One of the three biggest life challenges for people is money (with the other two being health and love).

Naturally, I see the effects of the distortions from all three of these life areas quite often in working with my clients who are entrepreneurs desiring business transformation.

I'm honored to be able to translate their messages into sometimes dramatic change. The key is remembering that's all these messages are... distortions.

Issues in any one of these areas are not a reflection on who you are intrinsically; instead, consider them an invitation to greater consciousness.

To make a living from who you are, and because your business can grow only as fast as you do, you have to make friends with your money. All of it... what you generate AND what you owe.

If money WERE your live, in-person, breathing and dynamic friend, would you treat it the way you have been up until now?

If not, keep reading...

AND, if you do keep reading, this is going to take a minute... there's a ton of info here for you.

As a result of working with a VIP client, I came up with some questions for a quick way to enhance your relationship with your money.

One of the exercises she did was to envision what her money looked like as a person. Her money was not tall, dark, and handsome. Instead, her money felt more like an icky diaper to be held at arm's length while holding her nose. Said that way, it seems obvious why she wasn't attracting more money, right?

A quick caveat—I'm NOT a financial professional!!! I'm not sure each and every one of the following has relevance to you and your situation either—these are truly just the basics to help you get started in building a better friendship with your money.

To REALLY get into your finances, I suggest you seek a financial professional. That said, the following may be enough to get you rolling in a new way. You may already be doing some of these and, in that case, bravo! If not, or if any of these cause you to feel a sting, a ping or an ouch (kinda like a whack upside the head or a drop in the pit of your tummy), know that now is your choice to do something different.

Ok… here goes…! :+)

Money Friendship
Self-Quiz and Action Plan

Work through this at a pace comfortable for you. This is not about being perfect. Instead, this is about creating a new relationship with money as an entrepreneur based on the facts of what IS in your life right now. Once you see the contrast between where you are and what you want, you can create it with focused right action.

Credit Report

- Have you ever seen your credit report?
- If yes, was it more than 18 months ago?

If you said no or it's been more than 18 months, it's time to get a new credit report.

When you do get your credit report, go through it to make sure all the information listed in it is correct. There are three credit bureaus: Equifax, TransUnion, and Experian. There are some services that compile the reports from all three bureaus into one to make it easier to read. As of this writing, CreditKarma.com and Privacy-Guard.com are worth checking out.

- Do you know your credit rating (or FICO score)?
- If yes, is it above 700?

If it's less than 700, put together a plan to get it to at least 700. This might mean correcting info on your credit report, paying off old balances, closing out defunct accounts or some other action.

When you have to update your credit report in any way, allow a good three months for that to show up on your credit report.

Also, remember any time you request financing from someone (for a car, credit card or other type of loan), that request will show up on your credit report and could adversely affect your credit rating.

When you have requested credit and been refused, that will show up on your credit report as a negative too.

Installment Agreements

- Do you know how much money you owe and to who or what institution?

- Is it written down in one place so you can easily reference and update it each month?

- Do you know how much interest you are paying to each debtor?

When you don't know any of the above, you've got some homework to do.

When you are paying more than 15% interest, it's time to negotiate that interest level because you're paying a lot of money in interest. (Or you might be able to get 0% cards and transfer the balances to save paying interest.)

- Are you late on making any scheduled payments?

- If yes, how much are the late payment fees you pay each month?

- If yes, are you more than 30 days late? (At 60 days late, that late payment will adversely affect your credit rating.)

- Also if yes in being late with a payment, what can you do to get back into integrity with this payment(s)?

Money Systems

- Do you balance your checkbook(s) regularly?
- Do you have an online bookkeeping system that is synced with your checking account and credit cards?
- Do you have a bookkeeper for your business?
- Do you have a regular accountant or CPA for your business?
- Do you have any outstanding receivables or collections you are waiting to receive from clients?
- If yes, do you have procedures in place in your business for Accounts Receivable?
- Have you checked the rates you're paying to process credit cards as a merchant to see if your current rates are competitive?
- Do you pay your bills online as much as possible? This saves not only postage and drive time to the post office but also provides a digital trail of your payment and minimizes risk of postal theft or bank fraud when your check payment is stolen.

Also, when you're using PayPal or another similar service, you may reach a point of diminishing returns; that is, when you make money consistently and process that through a money service, you could be paying more than you need to for processing fees. Ask your banking professional to run an analysis for you to see if it makes sense to get a merchant account.

Taxes

- Are you caught up in reporting your taxes through the most current year?
- Do you make estimated tax payments on time for this year?
- If your business has a corporate entity structure, are you paying payroll taxes on time?

If you expect to get a refund at the end of the year, something is wrong! You're giving your money to the government and letting them use it vs. keeping it and investing it to work for you. Despite common thinking, it is NOT better to pay in too much throughout the year. Adjust your payments accordingly.

Budget

- Do you know off the top of your head what you need to live on each month?
  If no, take time to sit down and write out your needs to calculate that number. The Universe cannot bring you what you don't know you need.
- Do you have a business budget in place each month for your fixed and variable expenses?
- Do you have a personal budget in place each month for your fixed and variable expenses?
- Do you honor your budget(s)?

Debt

- Do you have payment plans in place for each debt you owe?
- Do you pay more than the minimum required for each debtor each month?

A rule of thumb is to make at least the minimum payment plus the interest for that month to ensure you are making progress on the principal loan with that debtor. It can be a small stretch that pays you back in reducing the time and amount needed to repay that loan.

- Do you pay the minimums on all loans EXCEPT the debt with the highest interest being charged—then put the extra money you have toward that one to strategically eliminate the highest interest loan first (since it's costing you the most)? This is also called the avalanche method of debt reduction.
- Do you pay off the smallest debts first to get them out of the way, then move on to the bigger ones? This is called the snowball method of debt reduction.

Whichever method you choose (avalanche or snowball), make sure it feels motivating to you so you do it consistently over time.

Relationship with Money

- When you DO need to use credit, is it to make an investment in something that will pay you back or is it for basic living expenses? (If it's the latter, the simple solution is to just make more money!)
- Do you use mostly cash or cards to pay for things?
- Does digital money, like credit and debit cards, represent real money to you or do you feel like you can just spend it on anything without repercussion?

When digital money doesn't feel real, consider getting that money into your hands so you can physically spend it... you might have a greater appreciation for it.

- Do you have any savings?
- At what point do you feel like you're 'broke'—when you have $1,000 in the bank or $1? (You have to know where you feel abundant in order to keep your energy high.)
- Do you know how much money you make?

Some service-based entrepreneurs find it shocking that they actually make money about 25% of the time. The rest of their time is spent in administration, marketing, sales, operations, etc. Beyond that, their revenues also need to cover taxes, health insurance, vacation and more. Know how much money you want to make and charge accordingly to account for the 'hidden' costs of making money.

- Do you consistently have more month than money?

If you said yes, sit down immediately to come up with a strategy to bring in additional money. This is no time to be proud! Instead, focus on ways large and small that can bring you more money immediately; once you have your needs met, you can focus on longer-term, more strategic methods to bring in additional revenues.

- Are you bringing in enough money to live comfortably?

Remember, this is based on what you know you need each month. First, know your fixed expenses (your needs), then your wants (anything above a barebones budget), then your stretch abundance goal. Once you know those numbers, you have your financial range targets. Total the amount of money you currently know how to get and/or receive monthly; if there is a gap, do what you already know to do—come up with a plan to bring in money now.

In my life, I've had more of those moments than I can count... I've been a golf merchandiser, a house painter, a ballroom dance instructor, a resume writer, a copywriter, a professional belly dancer, an office cleaner, a garage sorter, a personal shopper, a mystery shopper... I did whatever I had access to in that moment to bring in additional cash. Along the way, I met new people and created new opportunities for myself that I never could have predicted in advance. Just remember whatever you do is only temporary. You might be surprised how much fun you have with it.

A Gift to Help You
Manifest Monthly

Simply by putting into place what you need to generate a living that is congruent with who you are, you can make friends with money really fast. (That's what I do and teach in working with my clients.)

To help you get congruent with your being and doing, honoring your gifts and making a living from who you are, remember that being in business is your highest calling made manifest through service.

It makes the world a better place.

And it makes you your best self to be and do it, whatever your thing is…

Whether or not you are actively in business or not, to help you manifest your money and clear up debt with focus and accountability, I have a special download for you. It's a two-page monthly budget. I call it a Monthly Money Manifesting Template:

lynnscheurell.com/monthly-template

Whether or not we ever actually meet or work together, I trust this has helped you get a fresh perspective on how to make friends with your money.

P.S.: An update on my client: in less than 24 hours, she has gotten an updated credit report, committed to upgrading her relationship with money and is feeling more freedom in her overall relationship with money than she's had in years… it goes to show that once you release what's holding you back, you can spring forward with clarity and ease.

In Closing

Money is a personal and complex relationship between you and all the parts of your life. Each person develops their own style, approach, and outcomes with money. It is a unique relationship that underscores many people's lives. Without money in today's world, it's difficult to feel like you have freedom to live your best life.

Every single person on the planet has the same 24 hours in a day; and yet, some people are so much more successful financially in that same amount of time as others. There are many theories around that by people much smarter than me—economists, financial professionals, even historians who track financial power through the ages. And there are those who inherit their money vs. earn it. Since you are reading this book, I am figuring that you are not independently wealthy and are earning your way to wealth. So what can you do better, more efficiently and/or more effectively with your time and attention to support your wealth? That is the question.

For me, there is one question that applies to literally every financial decision I make in life. It is the following question.

Is this moving me further toward or away from my life goals?

Obviously, if it is moving me away from my life goals, I need to do something different to course-correct. If I can't do anything, at least I have the awareness and can start 'seeding' new outcomes in incremental steps, including metaphysical insights.

I trust this book has helped surface insights and clarity around your relationship with money. My intention was to give you a plethora of tools and perspective so this book is valuable to you over time. (Many of my clients tell me that's part of the value of my work—that it is timeless and there is more to be gained upon re-listening to our sessions even years later.)

At any rate, I believe we live in an abundant Universe. You are not here to be anything less than wealthy by your own definition. Here's to actualizing your clarity and upshifting your relationship with the energy of your money.

Lynn

P.S.: Please drop me a line and let me know what you learned from this book—I'd love to hear and celebrate your momentum!

About the Author

Lynn Scheurell, writer, author, teacher, professional catalyst and Feng Shui practitioner since 1998, is an authority on making the most of human nature. She works with non-conformists, renaissance souls, visionaries and thought leaders in changing the world and getting paid for it through entrepreneuring.

By definition, a catalyst provokes significant change; this is what people expect in working with Lynn. She is an innovator and facilitator of the complex made simple.

Lynn's personal mission is to discover and illuminate truth through intuitive insights, understanding life energies and co-creative dialogue with her clients. Recognizing that all energy moves through the universe and is interconnected on all levels, a dynamic relationship occurs for each individual, their goals, and their environment at any given time. Feng Shui is that relationship.

By experiencing both their own and Lynn's intuitive and emotional intelligence, clients are able to explore the richness of their being and discover their best life. Accordingly, they are able to remove obstacles and design their environments using universal energetic principles to actualize potential opportunities and magnetize optimal life flow.

The most direct way to create change and movement is by assessing the situation, identifying the symptoms, looking at the sources of those symptoms, experiencing the shift of illumination, and creating a solution. Clients working with Lynn recognize her ability to "read" their internal and external environments, helping them discover and manifest their own desires through a tangible process that reflects their truths.

Lynn currently resides in Palm Springs, CA area. She considers herself to be a practical visionary, idea generator and facilitator of positive transformation through clarity consciousness. **LynnScheurell.com**

LinkedIn: linkedin.com/in/lynnscheurell/

Twitter: twitter.com/lynnscheurell

Instagram: instagram.com/lynnscheurell/

YouTube: youtube.com/user/mycreativecatalyst

Other Books
by the Author

You've Arrived!: A 5-Step System to Bypass Your Logical Mind, Activate Your Intuitive Potential and Gain Perfect Clarity For Your Business

Feng Shui for Entrepreneurs: Harnessing the Power of Your Environment for Business Success

Heal The Chakras Of Your Business: Adapt Ancient Wellness Systems For The Wealth Of Your Business Today

The Entrepreneurial Guidebook: How To Reach Your Potential, Help More People And Change The World

Printed in Great Britain
by Amazon

41868317R00126